SHOWTUNE

SHOWTUNE

A MEMOIR BY
JERRY HERMAN

with Marilyn Stasio

DONALD I. FINE BOOKS
New York

Donald I. Fine Books
Published by the Penguin Group
Penguin Books USA Inc., 375 Hudson Street,
New York, New York 10014, U.S.A.
Penguin Books Ltd, 27 Wrights Lane,
London W8 5TZ, England
Penguin Books Australia Ltd, Ringwood,
Victoria, Australia
Penguin Books Canada Ltd, 10 Alcorn Avenue,
Toronto, Ontario, Canada M4V 3B2
Penguin Books (N.Z.) Ltd, 182–190 Wairau Road,
Auckland 10, New Zealand

Penguin Books Ltd, Registered Offices:
Harmondsworth, Middlesex, England

First published by Donald I. Fine Books, an imprint of
Penguin Books USA Inc.

First Printing, November, 1996
10 9 8 7 6 5 4 3 2 1

All lyrics published by Jerryco Music Company.

Library of Congress Cataloging in Publication Data:
Herman, Jerry, 1933–
Showtune : a memoir / by Jerry Herman : with Marilyn Stasio.
p.   cm.
ISBN 1-55611-502-4
1. Herman, Jerry, 1933–   . 2. Composers—United States—
Biography.   I. Stasio, Marilyn.   II. Title.
ML410.H5624H47   1996
782.1′4′092—dc20
[B]   96-34210
CIP
MN

Printed in the United States of America
Set in Galliard
Designed by Irving Perkins Associates, Inc.

For Ruth

Introduction

∙ ∙

"There's just no tune
As exciting as a showtune in 2/4
When it's played, you can just tell
There's footlights everywhere
When it's played, you can just smell
The greasepaint in the air. . . ."

THAT LYRIC COMES from one of the first songs I ever wrote. It's called "Showtune," and it pretty much explains what Jerry Herman is all about.

I was about sixteen when I wrote that song, and it's obvious that I was madly in love with musical comedy. I still am. It is one of the few purely American art forms that we have—and we still do it better than anybody.

This book is really about my romance with the showtune. Even during periods like the 1970s, when showtunes became unfashionable, I never faltered in my love for that distinctive American sound. I stayed with it and helped keep it alive. And I always will.

I lived through an incredible age of the American musical that everybody today suddenly longs for—that remarkable period of the 1950s and 1960s when show after show after show opened on Broadway. I lived through all that, and like everybody else in the business in those days, I thought it would never end.

I was just a kid when I burst on the scene and had this crazy early success with three big musicals—*Milk and Honey, Hello, Dolly!,* and *Mame.* From that time until this very minute, my life has been an amazing roller-coaster ride of dizzying success followed by disappointing failure followed by more wild success.

When I was a little boy, my father used to take me on the roller coaster. I can still remember the thrill of those rides. Those deep, scary drops always seemed as exciting to me as those high, thrilling climbs. In the same way, I feel that when my life is at the bottom of the roller coaster, it is just as interesting as it is at the high points. Maybe even *more* interesting, in the case of a show like *Mack and Mabel,* which I once considered a failure and which has now just won a Best Musical award in London!

My personal story is also mixed up with the stories of the people I worked with, and with the tale of that era we all lived through. People like Carol Channing, Ethel Merman, Mary Martin, Gower Champion, Angela Lansbury, Robert Preston, Pearl Bailey, and so many others. Just naming their names calls back that magical time of the Broadway musical comedy. I even worked with some people you wouldn't expect, like Betty Grable, Ginger Rogers, Lucille Ball, Susan Hayward, and Dorothy Lamour.

That was a unique time in America, and we may never see anything like it again. The musical theater will go on, and the showtune will never die. But I don't think we will ever have that special kind of American entertainment in quite the same way.

So I guess my own story is also a piece of history. It was a golden era—and I had a wonderful chunk of it.

—JERRY HERMAN

ONE

"It's Today"

I REMEMBER WAKING up to the sun shining through my window. Not that you could see very much from my third-floor walkup in Greenwich Village—just the apartment building across the way. But when I woke up for the first time in my very own home at 6 East Tenth Street, I bolted out of bed and ran to the window to look out at this new world where I was going to start my new life.

No matter who you are or what kind of fabulous life you lead, you never forget the thrill of moving into your own place. There is nothing as exhilarating as that sense of independence, that feeling of beginning a marvelous adventure.

That's the way it was for me, anyway, in 1955 when I moved out of the very middle-class house in Jersey City where I had grown up with my mother and my father and my grandmother and moved into my first New York apartment, a $90-a-month walkup in a Village brownstone. It was only one room, very simple and unspectacular, with a little kitchenette and a bathroom, and that's it. There was barely room in this place for my mother's spinet and the sofa I had brought from home. But I was in heaven because it was *mine*. I had my piano, I had my briefcase, I had my home.

And all of it said to me: "You are on your own, kid. You are on your way!"

That first morning, the possibilities for a life and a career seemed endless. I already had my first job, playing piano in a Village supper club, and this very day I had an interview with a real theater producer to talk about some revue material I wanted to turn into a show. But first, I was going to explore my neighborhood and find a supermarket so I could stock my tiny refrigerator. And on the way to my interview I wanted to stop in at Paul Stuart's to look at the new spring suits. At that point in my life, all I could afford to do was look.

Standing there at my sunny window and planning these exciting adventures, I felt like I was celebrating a very important holiday in my life. It wasn't my birthday, or New Year's Eve, or the Fourth of July; but as my mother used to say: "It's today!" In our house, that was always reason enough to celebrate.

I GREW UP in this very warm, happy home that was full of music. My father played the saxophone and my mother played the piano. Mom was also a whiz at the accordion, so when I started playing the piano, we had a trio. Every night after dinner we would go into the living room and play Irving Berlin and Rodgers and Hart songs until they came out of our ears. This was our family fun—and no one can tell me that it didn't rub off on my own musical style.

My father was a gym teacher in the New York City school system and for a time, my mother also taught school. In the summers my parents ran Stissing Lake Camp, this popular children's camp that they owned in upstate New York. The camp was located in Pine Plains, which is very pretty country in the foothills of the Berkshire Mountains, and from the time I was six years old until I turned twenty-one, this was where I spent my summers.

Every June, the three of us would go up with a group of workmen to open the camp. The men would put two rafts out on the water, one for the boys' camp and one for the girls' camp on the other side of the lake. My mother would go through the cabins, cleaning and polishing everything and stocking the kitchen. My job was changing the lightbulbs. I would go around the entire camp with this big basket of lightbulbs. That was our summer vacation, getting this place ready for three hundred kids who would be arriving in three weeks. I suppose it was work, but my parents made it fun, wonderful fun.

As an only child, I was kind of a loner when I was a kid. But every summer those three hundred kids at Stissing Lake Camp became the brothers and sisters that I didn't have at home. Many of the campers would come back year after year, which is how I was able to form some indelible friendships from an early age. With my shy nature, I could have turned out to be a *real* loner. I didn't, because summer camp took me out of my shell. The whole camp experience gave me a huge family for two months of every year and some friendships that I have held on to for a lifetime.

My parents didn't want me to be singled out because I was the owners' son, so I was always treated like just another camper at Stissing Lake. I lived in a cabin with the other campers, made up my own cot, and did everything the other kids did.

The only difference was that I would always rather play the piano than play basketball. So that's what I did. Every night after dinner, I would go into the social hall, sit down at the piano, and play songs for three hundred voices. When it got dark, we would sit around a fire and sing "Hail, Hail, the Gang's All Here" and all those other easy, melodic songs that kids sing at camp. I am talking about those real *rousers* that anybody could sing once they'd heard them a few times.

Although it didn't occur to me when I was writing *La Cage aux Folles*, "The Best of Times" is very much like those camp songs that we used to sing around the fire every summer at Stissing Lake. You could probably say that about a lot of the upbeat, feel-good songs I write. That actually makes me smile, because those summer nights when I sat at the piano playing songs that people loved to sing were some of the happiest times of my life.

ONE THING I did not do at camp was join in the dancing. People are always surprised when I tell them that I don't know how to dance. I have excellent rhythm and it's obvious that I love to write dance music. But I have never been a dancer, not even a social dancer, because I was always the one sitting at the piano. To my mind, I was doing something better than dancing. I was making the music so other people could dance.

There was more to it than that, of course, and now that I've brought up the subject of dancing, I have to admit that it's a painful one. Even today, at formal affairs and big social events, I am very conscious of sitting all by myself at the table when everybody else gets up to dance.

As a child, I was small for my age and terribly shy. I was a good swimmer and I loved hiking. But I didn't always do what the other kids were doing, at the same time that all the other kids were doing it. When everyone else was playing baseball, I was playing the piano. And when I got to be a teenager and everyone else was dancing, I was still playing the piano. Like sports, dancing was something I stayed away from because I never felt comfortable doing something that I couldn't do really well.

Maybe that's why that whole "Dancing" sequence is one of my favorite things in *Hello, Dolly!* I am charmed by the dancing lesson and the way that Dolly is able to take a clod like

Cornelius and turn him into a dancer. That's why I wrote that song, because it was really *me* wanting to dance and not having the guts to try it. I needed a Dolly Levi to make me get out there and just do it. Just *dance*.

It wasn't so bad when I got to college and started playing the piano at fraternity and sorority dance parties. Playing music was something that I could do very well, and in college I found people who appreciated my musical talent and admired me for it. In four years of college I never got out on the dance floor. But I was always at the piano, where I felt like some-body—just the way I did during those wonderful summers at Stissing Lake.

THE HAPPY ATMOSPHERE of my childhood had a big influence on my work, as well as my life. My parents were musical comedy lovers who lived for the theater. They went to a Broadway show almost every Friday night, and when I was old enough they took me with them, the same way that families today go to the movies together.

A theater ticket in those days cost $4.40—funny how I can still remember that price. We didn't sit in the best seats in the house; but just the same, we were in the theater to see *Finian's Rainbow* and *Brigadoon* and *Call Me Mister* and *Oklahoma!* I was taken to *everything*. It was our thing to do together, as a family.

One night, my parents took me to the Majestic Theater to see *Annie Get Your Gun*. That show had the most profound effect on me, starting with that larger-than-life lady who was on stage belting out songs like home runs. Ethel Merman ab-solutely did it for me. I got a load of that great lady and I was gone! I said to myself, "Okay, kid, this is it. This is the most exciting thing in the whole world. It just doesn't get any better than this."

I was only about fourteen at the time and pretty impression-
able. Listening to that Irving Berlin music coming from the
stage, I suddenly got the feeling that his music was like a personal *gift* to me, from a man I had never met. I remember
thinking what a great joy that must be, to be able to give the
gift of music to people.

When we got home from the theater that night I went
straight to the piano and played "They Say That Falling in
Love Is Wonderful" and "There's No Business Like Show
Business" and snatches of other songs I remembered. I have
this crazy musical ear, so I was always able to do things like
that.

My mother used to tell this story about this one day when
just the two of us were in the house and she suddenly heard
music coming from the piano. She came to the top of the stairs
and called down, "Who's there with you, Jerry?" She knew we
were alone, and when I didn't answer her, she ran down the
stairs—and there was this six-year-old kid, sitting at the piano
and playing the Marines' Hymn, "From the halls of Monte-
zuma . . ." With two hands, no less.

According to my cousin Millicent, I got this gift when I was
still in my mother's womb. It was July 10, 1931, and Millicent,
who was eleven years old at the time, was visiting our house
when my mother suddenly started going into labor. Everyone
got very excited and started rushing her down the stairs and
out the front door. But my mother stopped them and said,
"Just give me a minute." She went into the living room, sat at
her piano, and played a song.

My father, my grandmother, everybody was running around
getting hysterical. Here was this woman with labor pains playing the piano. "Ruth," my grandmother said, "please tell me
why you are doing this to yourself." And my cousin Millicent
heard my mother say, "I want my child to love music."

So I have always had this ability to hear a song and transfer it instantly to my fingers. But what happened the night I saw *Annie Get Your Gun* was different. I remember sitting at the piano, running over those melodies, and saying to myself: "This is the most incredible feeling in the world, playing these showtunes. I want to make this kind of music. I *have* to do this."

I don't know any other way to say it: I fell in love with musical comedy when I was very young, and it is still my greatest passion. I go to opera, I go to ballet, I go to drama and comedy. But when I go to a musical and they start the overture, my heart leaps up.

I give all the credit to my parents for exposing me to theater music. In those early years, I was being trained without being trained. The funny thing is, my parents didn't know they were doing that. It was just their fun—our family fun—something they happened to love.

Which is not to say that there wasn't a major family crisis when I later announced that I was going to write Broadway musicals for a living. My father was a very practical and pragmatic person who wanted his son to be assured of a steady income. He and my mother had been married during the Depression, so his attitude was understandable.

Luckily for me, I had a very romantic, glamorous mother who thought the theatrical life was the most exciting life in the world. In some ways my parents were perfect opposites, and on this issue of my career they were on opposite sides. She pushed me and he tried to keep me back. And it became a source of tension in the house.

MY MOTHER, RUTH Herman, was a gorgeous woman and I just adored her. With her dark, flashing eyes and wonderful smile, she looked very much like Ruth Roman and Barbara Stanwyck in their Hollywood heyday. My mother was also the real musician of the family, as a pianist and a singer who had her own radio show before she married my father. Mom didn't have any great theatrical aspirations, but she was a great performer and a brilliant party-thrower and the most important influence in my life.

In a sense, my mother is in every song I write. But there is one song in particular that I will always associate with her.

It was 1965, and I had just got the assignment to do *Mame*. I already had this huge hit, *Hello, Dolly!*, running on Broadway, so it was a very high point in my life and I was extremely happy to have this new assignment. But just the same, there is nothing more terrifying than the first day you sit down to write a musical.

So there I was, with this empty piece of paper on the piano. My first thought was: "Oh, my God, I have two years of this ahead of me, and I don't know where to start!" Then I thought: "Well, I better just start at the beginning and get that opening number done." I had already worked out a rough structure with my collaborators Jerome Lawrence and Robert E. Lee. So I knew that there was going to be a song at the beginning of the show, and I knew that it was going to take place at a big party.

Well, I *hate* writing party songs. What can you say about a party? "Have a good time, everybody"? Boring! It is also the hardest kind of song for me to write because I get my musical ideas from character, not from situation. Tell me to write a song about a garden and I really won't know what to do. But tell me to write a song about a woman who is tending that garden because she doesn't have a lover, and I know exactly how to do it.

What I had to do for that opening number of *Mame* was to somehow personify this party. I had to write about this glamorous woman who was *giving* this party. And then, whoosh! I had this instant flash of memory from some other place and time, to the house where I grew up.

I remembered coming home from school—I must have been seven or eight years old at the time—and finding my mother in the kitchen, making these elaborate hors d'oeuvres for a party. Now, you have to understand that I grew up in a house of parties. My mother had her bridge club parties, and both she and my father had their Saturday night club parties. And they were always throwing these absolutely *mad* theme parties, with costumes and music and all kinds of wonderful food.

I remembered saying to my mother: "I didn't know we were having company tonight. It's only Tuesday, so what's the occasion?" And I remembered that she just smiled and said, "It's today!"

Sitting at that piano so many years later, staring at that empty piece of paper, I suddenly got gooseflesh. Even now, I can still remember that *feeling* I got when my mother smiled and said, "It's today!"

That became my opening number for *Mame*.

> "Light the candles
> Get the ice out
> Roll the rug up
> It's today!
> Though it may not be anyone's birthday
> And though it's far from the first of the year
> I know that this very minute
> Has history in it
> We're here! . . ."

That song is *total* Ruth Herman, and it was one of the rare times when I felt that some truly special spark from the past had come to me.

9

* * *

THE SAD THING is that my mother never got to see the show. I lost her to cancer when I was twenty-one and she was only forty-four. That was the great tragedy of my life. Ruth Herman was beautiful and young and funny and I adored her. She was my closest friend and I thought I was going to have her at every opening night and make her proud of me. But she never even lived to see my first Broadway show, *Milk and Honey.* She never saw a single show of mine on Broadway.

My mother died of cancer of the jaw in 1954. She had gone to the dentist for her first tooth extraction, which made her very upset because she had such gorgeous teeth and she hated to lose one. When the wound didn't heal, the dentist sent her to a specialist who found it was cancer. She was operated on, but the disease got worse and worse. It was mercifully brief for her, but I remember how upset she was because the disease had disfigured her beautiful face. It was a horrible, horrible time—the lowest time of my life.

I know that this sounds like a big cliché—a gay boy who loves his mother—but my loving relationship with my mother happens to have been a *huge* part of my life. Ruth Herman was the first and maybe the most important of the influences that shaped me. To understand my years with my mother is to understand *me* better.

It is sometimes hard for me to realize that I have lived a lifetime without this person. But at least it doesn't pain me to think about her, because I have only happy thoughts of her. I never had good periods and bad periods with Mom, the way I had up times and down times with Dad. My memories of my mother are completely wonderful. She still brings me joy.

* * *

THERE IS ALSO a song that I associate with my father, but the story behind that one is more complicated, because my relationship with Harry Herman was also more complicated. I guess it was this very classic case of an only child who adored his mother, who didn't really like his father, and who turned out to be gay.

I had a real rah-rah gym instructor for a father, an athletic man who wanted his son to be an athlete, too. What he got was this son who sat at the piano. Dad didn't know how to deal with me, and I didn't know how to deal with him. There were times when we were like two strangers living in the same house.

This caused a lot of stress in the family and made my growing up a little rocky. I hated to be the cause of argument between my parents, but my mother would always back me up. She would take my side by saying: "Leave the kid alone. Let him do what's natural for *him* to do. He is finding his own way and he's doing something wonderful."

But my father wouldn't listen. At camp, he was always trying to get me out on the baseball field. I was a stubborn kid and I wouldn't go. I would say to him: "Look, Dad, I don't want to play baseball because I don't know how to do it well. I don't throw a ball well and I don't catch well and I feel uncomfortable in front of all the other kids. Why can't you just let me do something that I *can* do, something that you can really be proud of?"

I was trying to tell him that when I was on the baseball field I was nobody. But when I played the piano, I was *somebody*. He never understood.

One day when I was about ten years old, I wanted to go to the camp social hall and play the piano. My father insisted that I had to play in this baseball game. In front of these hundreds of kids, he dragged me onto the field and put me in left field position. I stood there in this huge, open field, and I wouldn't move. At one point, the ball came right to me and I just stood there. The ball landed right at my feet and I just stood there. Hundreds of kids were screaming. But still I stood there.

I suppose I could have done it for my father—just that one day. But I wanted him to know that I was going to have no part of this. I also wanted him to know that he was not going to do this to me ever again.

AND THEN, ONE summer, my father finally let me put on a show.

I must have been around seventeen or eighteen, because I was going to be a director that summer and live in the guest house. Before we left for the lake, I went to the Drama Book Shop and bought a copy of *Finian's Rainbow*. When we got to camp I cut down the script and worked all summer on staging the show as a big event in the social hall.

It was a very ambitious production for a camp show. I made my father buy me lighting equipment and we had painted scenery, costumes, props, the works. I used all the older kids for the major roles and we had a big chorus. It was a wild success—such a wow that everyone wanted to come back next year to do another show. And we did, for the next several summers.

Those were the years that I loved. My mother was happy, my father was happy, and I had finally found my identity. I was also having the time of my life learning the structure of the Broadway musical comedy. Because that's exactly what I was doing, without realizing it—learning how a good show is constructed.

By the next season, I had turned my father's successful athletic camp into an even more successful dramatic camp. The show we put on that second summer was *A Tree Grows in*

Brooklyn. It starred a little girl named Alice Borden, who would play a big role in my life. That show I did with Alice rivaled the productions of the summer stock theater in the next town.

It had taken eighteen years of my life, but I had finally succeeded in making my father enormously proud of me. After my mother died, he even wanted me to take over the camp. I turned him down, but years later I came to realize that it was actually very kind and generous of him to make that offer. Dad wasn't trying to stop me from doing what I wanted to do with my life. He was just trying to ensure my future—and to express his love for me.

After my mother died, I became very soft about my father. Once I saw how much he missed her and realized how lost he was without her, my whole attitude about him changed. By the time he got married again, my own life was in order, and I liked his new wife very much. There was nothing to be gained by holding on to the old, bad feelings, so I decided to let all that stuff go.

My father and I ended up good friends, real pals. I have to say that I did it as much for myself as for him, but it was still an important early lesson for me. I have always been proud of myself for being able to change my attitude toward my father.

I am sure that I have put Harry Herman into my music, in the same way that I have used Ruth Herman's personality and philosophy. There is a little of Harry in Horace Vandergelder, although my father was much more like Phil Silvers than Horace. He was a funny, gregarious man—the real life of the party. Harry Herman was everybody's pal, the sort of person who would slap you on the back. In the early days, he was a social director in the mountains, which is how he met my mother.

The song of mine that I most associate with my father is the title song from this 1954 show that nobody's ever heard of: *I Feel Wonderful*. I was very young and I don't even want to talk about the caliber of the material, which was stuff I wrote in college. The important thing about this show is that my father supported me on it.

I was fresh out of college and my mother was still alive when I decided to do this off-Broadway musical revue at the Theatre De Lys. My father took it upon himself to finance the show. He went around to all the businessmen he knew and said to them: "Look, I only need a hundred dollars from you—and a hundred dollars from you and another hundred dollars from *you*—and it will help my kid out." *I Feel Wonderful* was a nothing show, but I will always associate it with my father because it represented Harry's emotional support of me and the real turnaround in our relationship.

SONG ASSOCIATION IS a funny thing, because that is *not* how I sit down to write a song. My way of writing is to immerse myself in the particular character whose thoughts and feelings I am musicalizing, even if he or she is personally unfamiliar to me. Some of my greatest challenges have been trying to write songs for people and situations that are completely foreign to me. But once a song is written, it should be accessible to everyone. No matter how obscure or unfamiliar the subject, I want everyone who hears a song of mine to be able to identify with it.

Take a song like "If He Walked Into My Life," from *Mame*. Audiences were very moved when that song was first sung by Angela Lansbury in the Philadelphia tryout. Now, at the point in the show where that song comes in, the audience was interested in Mame Dennis and her nephew, Patrick, because they liked them. But the real reason they were moved was because the song said something to them about their *own* lives.

I don't think there is a human being—certainly not any human being that I would want to know—who doesn't look back on some relationship and wonder: "If I had to do it all over again, would I make the same mistakes?" That is what that song makes us ask ourselves, and it is one of the most human things in the world. The secret of writing a moving song is to touch an emotion that everyone shares.

I'm no different myself, because that song makes me think of my grandmother, who lived with us for years during my growing-up. She was a real tough European lady who came over to America on a cargo ship from Minsk, a town on the Russian-Polish border. She was funny and adorable, and she was a major figure in our household.

I can best describe my "Bubi" by recalling a conversation she had at our kitchen table with me and my girlfriend, Joan Sue Cohen, a lovely Southern girl I had met at Stissing Lake. When the subject of marriage came up, my grandmother gave this advice to Joan Sue: "The only way you'll ever be able to trust your husband is if you cut it off and keep it in your pocketbook."

My grandmother was the Old World and my mother, who was born in Manhattan and was always in the very height of fashion, was the New World. But you could see the two worlds come together in their cooking—my grandmother's wonderful Jewish dish next to my mother's wonderful American dish. They were different in many ways, but they had fun together and they loved each other very much.

My grandmother lived many years longer than my mother. After Ruth was gone, my grandmother and I lived together in my parents' house, so I knew her very well. But I don't think that I realized at the time how difficult it had been for my grandmother to lose her daughter. We expect to lose our parents, we are all programmed for that eventual loss. But it must be terrible for a mother to lose her child, because that is a loss you don't anticipate.

When I thought about it years later, it seemed to me that my grandmother's loss must have been even greater than mine. But my own grief was so great that I think I didn't pay enough attention to my grandmother's grief, and I am sorry now that I was not more sensitive to her feelings.

I am not saying that I was thinking of my grandmother when I wrote that song. It's only later that you see where some of those emotions came from. And that's what helps me remember all the good times and the bad times, all the special people who were part of my music—and my life.

· ·

TWO

"I Feel Wonderful"

I NEVER TOOK my songwriting seriously, until Frank Loesser and the Mother Mafia changed my life.

In my home, music was an important part of our lives, so when I started writing my own songs my family was delighted and they all encouraged me. But I never thought of songwriting as anything but a hobby. My head told me that music is wonderful entertainment and great fun—you just don't take it seriously as a career.

So when it was time for college, I went to my other love, which was the field of architecture and design. My parents were very pleased with my decision and they were happy to pay my tuition to the Parsons School of Design. I was living at home and going to Parsons and I was loving the whole thing because I was being very creative.

One afternoon when I came home from school, my mother said: "You know, I have a friend in my bridge club who has a friend, and the brother of this friend of my friend knows Frank Loesser."

I don't remember exactly who knew who, but the Mother Mafia had it all figured out. Anyway, Ruth said: "I want you to play your stuff for him."

"You're my mother," I told her. "Of course *you* think my songs are good." I told her I wasn't interested in making a fool of myself in front of Frank Loesser.

Well, she gave me such a look! I can see her face right now. She just looked at me and said, "Would you please waste a half hour of your life?" That was exactly how she phrased it, and she cracked me up. I loved her sense of humor, and of course she was right. What could it hurt? So she set up this meeting.

My friend Phyllis Newman comes in here.

Phyllis lived four blocks from me and our families went to the same community center. She was a singer, she was beautiful, and she was a pal. We used to sit around and sing songs together after school.

Phyllis and I had this pact. If she ever needed an accompanist to go to an audition, I would go with her, and if I ever needed a singer when I was playing my songs, she would go with me.

So Phyllis and I went off with my little suitcase of songs to meet the great Frank Loesser. I was scared to death, but he turned out to be a fascinating man. He was colorful, he was salty, and he had a very vivid way of getting his thoughts across. He was only supposed to give me a half hour of his time, but after we played him a few of my songs, he shut the door and spent the rest of the afternoon with me.

The first thing he did was to take out this big drawing pad and colored marking pencils. He held the pad horizontally and drew this rough sketch of a freight train. First he drew the locomotive, with little puffs of smoke coming out of the smokestack. Then he drew all these boxcars in different colors. And then he put on the caboose—in red.

My eyes were popping out of my head. I couldn't imagine what he was up to.

"A song is like a freight train," he said. "It has to have a locomotive, which is the bold idea that first arrests your ear and propels you into the rest of the song."

I don't remember what examples he used, but here's the locomotive from one of Loesser's own songs: "I'm gonna get you on a slow boat to China." That's a great first line, and it does exactly what he says it should.

"The whole body of the song has to follow that first, fascinating idea," he said. "Like the different colors of the boxcars, what follows can be about many things, but they all have to go where that locomotive is going. Then comes the most important thing, the red caboose that ends the song with a twist, a little surprise."

Now, listen for the little red caboose on *his* song: "I'm gonna get you on a slow boat to China—all by myself, alone."

Mr. Loesser said that most of my own songs already had cabooses. But he wanted to make sure that I understood the principle of what I had done. He also made me promise that I would always remember to hook on the caboose, because that's what makes a good song. I never forgot that lesson.

At the end of our talk, he leaned back in his chair and looked at me. "What are you doing in design school?" he asked. "Why aren't you writing music?" I told him I was very *good* at design. "Just the same," he said, "I want you to tell your parents that I think you should try songwriting. It's a tough field, but I think you can make it. There is genuine talent here."

It's amazing, the things you can learn—and retain—from a good, strong, simple image like that train image that Frank Loesser gave me.

I did something like that myself recently, when I was in Sacramento working on *Tune the Grand Up*. That revue of my work had been running for two years in San Francisco when a new producer decided to book it into the *Delta King,* a show-boat docked in Sacramento Harbor. I went up to coach the new cast, and the first thing I realized was that they were doing all the numbers with exactly the same level of passion and intensity.

"Okay, let's stop," I told them. "Every song in this show has a different color. I am not going to teach you the songs, because you know the songs. I am going to teach you the different *colors* of the songs."

Then I took them through the songs, one by one. " 'Big Time,' from *Mack and Mabel,* is a big, hot, exciting show-tune," I told them. "You are singing it like a pink song. This is not a pastel song. This is a very out-front, passionate statement about people who are determined to make it big. This is a red song. Think fire-engine red."

Then came "It Only Takes a Moment," which is a pink song. It's sweet and it's quiet and it's loving. It doesn't have the same kind of energy as "Big Time." When we got to "If He Walked Into My Life," I told them the song was indigo, a very deep, rich shade of blue-violet. And when they got to "Bosom Buddies," I said, "Bright yellow! This is vaudeville—sell it!"

Well, they were fascinated. You'd think I was giving them stock-market tips.

WHEN I GOT home after seeing Frank Loesser, I was so starry-eyed that I walked around bumping into things. You are talking about a seventeen-year-old kid here. At the dinner table, I had to draw the train for my parents and give them the whole talk.

Mom, of course, was ecstatic. "What have you got to lose if you try this for a couple of years?" she told me. "You will always have your room in this house, and I will always slip you a couple of bucks for a good meal."

My father's viewpoint was: "You could starve in an attic somewhere with this. Why don't you come in with me on the children's camp?" I knew how much the camp meant to my father. But I got up the courage to ask him to help me do what *I* wanted to do—instead of what *he* wanted me to do. He thought about that and he didn't like it much, but he finally said, "Okay."

So I left Parsons after I finished my first year and went looking for a college that was known for its theater department.

I HAVE TO say right here that *any* college would have been better than high school. If you want to color my high-school years, you'd have to color them gray: I went. I did my work. I came home.

I had very few friends in high school. When everyone else was playing ball after school, I would come home and go straight to the piano.

One reason I was so uncomfortable in school was because I was two years younger than the other kids in my class. That was because of this terrible system we had in the Jersey City schools that let you skip grades if you did well in class. I was also small for my age, so no matter what class I was in, I was always the shrimp.

But it wasn't just my height and age, it was my whole personality. I was a loner as an adolescent, and I don't think it was because I was gay because I didn't even know it then. Oh, I must have sensed inwardly that there was something a little different about me. I might even have felt an attraction for an older classmate. But none of this was anything that I could have verbalized—or even dared to think about.

At this point in my life, my sexual feelings were all very

repressed, which was typical for the late 1940s. All I knew then was that I was happier coming straight home from school and going to my security blanket—my mother's piano.

The funny thing, though, was that the songs I wrote in high school were so *happy*. All those early attempts at songwriting were my way of aping the happy sentiments and the sunshine world of a musical comedy.

I remember this little musical I wrote when I was fifteen or sixteen. It was called *Step Right Up* and it had this sappy story about a guy and a girl at a carnival. My friend Phyllis Newman played the girl. If you heard it today, you would fall on the floor laughing. Only someone like Frank Loesser would see any merit in those silly songs.

So I was writing all those bright, happy showtunes. But I wasn't a happy kid. I was lonesome.

Mom and Dad were really worried about me. They tried everything to make me more outgoing. They were the king and queen of this very active Jewish community center we had in Jersey City, and they made me go to certain social events. I hated it.

I remember my mother practically *forcing* me to go to this dance class to learn social dancing. I went along to please her, but I felt so awkward that I pleaded with her not to make me go back. I actually *begged* her. I was so pathetic that she gave in.

I never felt like I belonged at those social events the way my parents did. I guess that dance class was the beginning of understanding for me. It was the first time I realized that there was something different about me—that I didn't quite fit in.

I *DID* FEEL that I fit in at college.

The University of Miami had a very avant garde theater department for that time. You didn't just sit in the classroom and you didn't just work in your own field. You also learned how to act, direct, and design a show. In my first year at school, I played Og, the leprechaun in *Finian's Rainbow*.

You also had to work in the costume room and the prop shop and you had to learn how to light a show. "I am going to be a songwriter," I remember saying. "What in the world do I need to know about lighting to write songs?"

Years later, I found out. We were working on *Mame* with Tharon Musser, who is the great lighting lady of all time. Tharon was having a hard time lighting Angela Lansbury for her solo of "If He Walked Into My Life." She tried this, she tried that, but nothing looked quite right.

I sat next to Tharon for a while without saying a word. Then, very quietly, I said, "Why don't you try an amber gel? It's autumn and she's in the country in Connecticut and the scene needs something warm, like an amber or a flesh tone."

Well, she looked at me with the strangest expression on her face. I could actually see her thinking, "Oh, sure. Now the *songwriter* thinks he's the lighting expert." But she picked up her microphone and told her technician in the light booth, "Try an amber gel on Miss Lansbury." Then she added a gobo, which made the lights look like swirling leaves, and the scene was absolutely gorgeous.

COLLEGE GAVE ME an enormous boost socially. It took me out of my scared-bunny hole and made me feel more comfortable about meeting people. When my parents and I were looking at schools, something in me said: "I need to break out. I need to join a fraternity and do varsity shows. *I need to make friends.*"

On the very first day of school I met Carol Dorian, and we became best friends for the rest of our lives.

There were ten thousand students at that school, which absolutely overwhelmed me. I was not used to that sort of scene, and on that first day I was petrified. But then I met Carol. We walked together to one of our classes and we started to talk. I found out that she was a singer and she found out that I wrote music. Something clicked for us, and from that moment, we became brother and sister.

Carol married Bob Dorian, a fraternity brother of mine, and the three of us remained the closest of friends. They were at my side through all the good things and stuck by me through all the bad things. They were my family.

College was a glorious experience that broke me out of my shell as an introverted only child. I belonged to this very straight fraternity where I was very well liked, and I had a girlfriend. Her name was Sally Singer, and we were *the* in-couple on campus. I even got to do the big varsity show—with a cast of ninety and a revolving stage!

That came about because the fraternities at my school had an annual musical competition, and in my freshman year my fraternity elected me to write our skit. I wrote this musical sketch about a university on another planet—and we won the trophy. The second year, I got more ambitious. We had a full orchestra, we had the most elaborate sets—and we won again. The next year, we won again.

By the fourth year, the other fraternities and sororities decided that it was foolish to continue this. So they junked the competition and *asked* me to put on the big varsity show. We did this lavish production at the Dade County Auditorium which was *the* event of the school year.

I was a big campus hero. I had learned how to use my talent, not just to write songs but to make a place for myself in the world. For the first time in my life, I felt that I really belonged.

The best thing was, I didn't become popular just because I wrote these shows that won prizes, or because I was the piano player at all the dances. I had made so many good friends that I couldn't just attribute my popularity to my music. I felt that the kids really liked me.

Not too long ago, I went back to the school for the official opening of a new theater that they had named for me. It gave me such a thrill to pull up to this brand-new, ultra-modern structure and then to look out the window and see my own name on it: the Jerry Herman Ring Theater.

The most exciting part of the whole trip, though, was working with college kids again, on a production of *Mame*, teaching them how to interpret the songs, find the emotion, get the laughs. We had a wonderful two-way rapport, and when I left I felt that I had succeeded in turning thirty teenage kids into permanent musical-comedy fans. These seventeen- and eighteen-year-old kids were a whole new generation that had just discovered my music, and it was the most gratifying feeling to know that my work would go on after me.

Looking back now, I can still say that those four years at the University of Miami were a *delicious* experience. I am also very thankful that my mother came down to see my student shows, because she never got to see any of my big Broadway shows. That still breaks my heart.

WHEN I LEFT the University of Miami, I was raring to go. The first thing I did was to rent a little theater and put on a revue of my college material. I called it *I Feel Wonderful* and the whole thing cost $15,000.

That's the show my father rounded up the backers for when we brought it to New York. To this day, I am still very touched by that. Here was this tough, macho man who had so desperately wanted a son who could play baseball and who was so disappointed in the son he got that we were almost enemies. And now he was going around being so proud and supportive.

I also feel good about that show because my mother was still alive to see it. That was such a happy time in my life. I really did feel absolutely wonderful.

When the show closed, I knew that I had to start supporting myself. I had to get a job. The one thing I knew how to do was play the piano, so I found an agent who got me a job playing cocktail piano in a New York club called the RSVP.

My job was to play very soft background music between sets, which suited me just fine. I had the perfect style for night-clubs because I loved to play ballads and I played them with feeling. I played all the Richard Rodgers, Cole Porter, and Irving Berlin songs that were ever written.

I was really in my element.

My FIRST JOB was also a fabulous learning experience because the headliner at the RSVP was Mabel Mercer.

I can't say, "Oh, Mabel and I were great friends. We used to go have drinks together." The woman didn't even know me. I was just this kid who made filler noise at the piano between her sets. But watching the great Mabel Mercer night after night was an extraordinarily valuable postgraduate course in song interpretation.

People will kill me for saying this, but Mabel Mercer was not a great singer. She was a lyricist's singer rather than a singer's singer. She acted those wonderful ballads she sang with such fierce passion and intelligence that you had to listen to every word. Because she was such a great actress, she became the definitive delineator of the *meaning* of a song.

The lyricist in me was absolutely fascinated by Mabel Mercer, who showed me how important it is to put *exactly* the right word on the right syllable. As someone who writes both music and lyrics, I am really two people. Sometimes I have to fight with myself over which craft is going to take precedence at a particular moment in a song. As a composer, I can write a musical line that I love; but if the lyricist in me feels that the line needs an extra syllable to get the meaning right, I have a very difficult decision to make.

If I hadn't listened hard to Mabel Mercer and learned how she delivered a song, I really don't think I could have written "Time Heals Everything." Years later, I had the wonderful satisfaction of hearing her sing my song at Town Hall. It was at the very end of her career and her voice was really shot, but I was devastated by the emotion she pulled out of that song and the deep meaning she conveyed. It was a beautiful moment for me, truly magical.

Thinking back, I guess that is why in my shows I have always gone with the actor who could deliver the meaning and the feeling of the song above the pure singer who could deliver the notes. Of course, it is always wonderful when you can get it all, like the great singing *and* the superb acting of George Hearn in *La Cage*. But if I had to make a choice, I would always go for the actor who gives me the guts and grit of a character, or the heartbreaking emotion of a song, or the brilliant timing of a line. That's what Mabel Mercer taught me.

I find this interesting about me, and maybe a little odd. But in my lifetime I have won more awards as a lyricist than as a composer, so maybe it is the lyricist in me who makes sure to pick actors for my shows.

BACK IN THE days when Mabel Mercer was the queen of the cabaret, there were so many posh little nightclubs in Manhattan that I can't even remember the names of all the clubs where I played. But I had a lovely career playing cocktail piano for a couple of years, and I remember those early jobs with fondness.

Being part of the cabaret circuit also gave me the chance to write special material for performers like Tallulah Bankhead,

Jane Froman, and Hermione Gingold. Hermione loved this funny number I wrote for her called "Best Gold." She made it her opening number. The lyrics were full of allusions to all the different kinds of gold there are in the world, like old gold, white gold, fool's gold. She always flashed the audience that mischievous smile of hers when she got to the last line: "But the *best* gold is *Ging*-gold!"

Sad to say, this was also the time when my mother became ill. When she died in 1954 I went into serious grieving for a whole year. I stopped doing everything. I was a basket case. My father and my grandmother didn't know what to do with me. At one point, I think my father was afraid that I would never come back to myself.

I knew that I needed help to get through this disastrous time of my life, but I didn't *want* help. This was before therapy became the socially acceptable thing to do, so therapy was never discussed. I also felt that it was my job to pull myself up by my own bootstraps. I considered it a very natural part of living to do what you have to do, even if you hate to do it. I still feel that way.

After a year of this terrible mourning for my mother, I decided to move to my first apartment in New York City. I wanted to be on my own. I was old enough and it was the right time.

Besides, my home was breaking up.

My father came to me about a year after my mother died and said, "What would you think if I took out Cousin Edna? She is very lonesome and so am I."

I appreciated that he asked me how I felt before he started to date Edna, whose husband had died about the same time as my mother. I was genuinely happy when they married the next year and moved to Miami, because I wanted Dad to find his own happiness and have someone who cared for him. But I hated to see my home disintegrating. When my father moved away and my grandmother went to live with her other daughter, my Aunt Belle, I was more alone than I had ever been before.

That's when my darling Aunt Belle stepped in. Belle was my mother's younger sister. She had a speaking voice and a manner like Beverly Sills—buxom and bubbly and full of fun. She always used to take me to the circus, and she adored me as much as I adored her.

My Aunt Belle, who was sweet and gentle, gradually became that special warm and loving person I could always talk to and share things with. If something lovely happened to me, the first person I would call was Aunt Belle. If someone told me they were going to sing a song of mine in a nightclub, I would tell Aunt Belle and she would run to see it. It was my bittersweet joy that, although my mother never got to see my shows, my Aunt Belle saw every single one.

THE DAY I moved into my first apartment was like the day I went away to school—a marvelous adventure.

I took my mother's piano to my little walkup on East Tenth Street, and some furniture from our house. My father, who was a jack of all trades and could fix anything, came over and built me this huge walk-in closet. I never had more than $100 a week to do anything with, so I was not exactly living high off the hog. But I had a smartly put-together apartment for someone who was just starting out.

I wanted to have my own life and I needed my independence—now, especially, because I had begun to sense what was happening with me sexually.

I was also writing more and more, and pretty soon I had a whole portfolio of songs. But I knew that no one was going to trust me to write a Broadway musical. It wasn't just my inexperience, it was the fact that I looked so much younger than my years. What producer would look at me and take me seriously?

In fact, when I went to meet the producer Kermit Bloomgarden, the first thing he said to me was: "I have to be honest with you. Can you see me investing millions of dollars in a musical and putting it on your shoulders?" He meant that I looked like a little boy. "Mr. Bloomgarden," I said, and I actually laughed when I said it, "I totally agree with you. I wouldn't do it, either."

Well, I had to admit that nobody was going to give me *My Fair Lady* to write. But that didn't mean I couldn't get around that my own way. I saw this revue craze going strong, so I kept on writing revue material until by 1958 I had a whole briefcase full of topical satirical songs.

The question was, what to do with them? I decided to make the rounds of all these little clubs in the Village.

Right now, I want to say that there is nothing more depressing than a seedy nightclub on West Fourth Street in the middle of the afternoon. You open this black door and the sun comes into this black room and it is truly hideous.

One afternoon I walked into this dark jazz club called the Showplace that I sort of sensed could use a shot in the arm. I went up to the proprietor and said: "I have a revue for you that could turn this place into what's happening uptown at the Upstairs at the Downstairs—and I can do it very, very inexpensively." I told him the whole thing would only cost $12,000 and I showed him the figures.

I guess this club wasn't doing very well, because the owner didn't throw me out. He sat me down at the piano and said, "Play me a couple of things."

I played him this song called "Skip the Opening Number," which was a satire on all those mindless opening numbers where the girls come out and kick. I played him a ballad, "I

Wish I Could Say." After a few more songs, he walked over to the piano and said, "You've got a deal."

WELL, I PUT the whole thing together myself and I called it *Nightcap*. And when I say "the *whole* thing," that's what I mean. I directed, I wrote sketches, and I played the piano.

I even did the set, which was a riot of ribbons and balloons and all those colorful, clichéd cabaret trappings. For our opening number, "Skip the Opening Number," I bought all these ribbons in bright jewel tones and I hung them with transparent clothespins from a thin nylon line. During the number, the performers pulled down the ribbons and balloons one at a time and packed them away in a trunk. At the end, they rolled the trunk away, leaving a black, empty stage.

And guess what I did for the opening of Act Two—a little number called "Showtune."

I tell you, it was like Mickey and Judy putting on a show. Phyllis Newman came in to do the choreography. So all I needed now was a cast of four brilliant performers who needed the work so badly they would go into this depressing little hole in the wall and work for minimum slave wages.

Phyllis also set up an audition for this young comedian she knew. So one day, up the three flights of my walkup and into my apartment came—Charles Nelson Reilly.

He was petrified, and that amazed me. In my whole life, nobody had ever been afraid of me. When I saw how nervous he was, I got him a Coke and I tried to make him feel comfortable.

"You are in a third-floor walkup," I said to him. "What could you possibly be nervous about?" He said, "I am not a good auditioner. I hate to audition." I said, "Then let's not call it an audition. Let's just sing some songs together and have a nice time."

Well, the only song he knew was "There But for You Go I" from *Brigadoon*, which is a very serious song. He was supposed to be auditioning for the comedy role, so I thought he was kidding. But when I went over to the piano, Charles Nelson Reilly very seriously sang this very serious song as an audition for a comedy role. I said to myself, anybody with this mad streak in him must be brilliant.

Then we started talking, and he made me laugh so hard, I had to hold myself. So I gave him the part and we became permanent friends.

Charles was a truly funny and original comic talent. After I got to know his style I wrote special song material for him. One of these songs, "Confession to a Park Avenue Mother," was a real showstopper. Charles was hilarious when he was nervous. So, I had him come out as this well-bred young man in a smoking jacket, holding a teacup and shaking with fear because he had to tell his snooty mother that he was in love with a West Side girl—a girl so declassée she had never eaten at La Grenouille.

> "If the stork in this tragic case
> Just had dropped her on Sutton Place
> For in every other way she's made to order
> But cruel fate had her conceived across the border. . . ."

Charles sang it like some terribly tragic lament. He was so funny, the audience screamed at every couplet.

THE SHOWPLACE WAS just a tiny little place—I think it seated seventy people—but we had an opening night and we had a press agent. Somehow that press agent got Richard Watts, Jr., the critic of the New York *Post*, to come down and review us. And he wrote us the most amazing notice: "Young Mr. Herman's revue, for which the term 'intimate' seems a bit too grandiose, is essentially of Broadway caliber and he is sure to wind up on the Main Stem in short order."

I didn't even know this until the next evening when I walked over to the theater and saw a crowd outside. I figured they were customers for the restaurant next door, and I got very upset because they were hiding the two billboards I had made for the front of the theater.

Very politely, I started to ask them to please step away from the front of the theater, so people could see that my show was playing there. That's when I realized that this whole crowd was waiting in line to buy tickets. That was my first experience with a crowd and a ticket line, and it is an indescribable feeling. I swear that it gives me goosebumps to remember it now.

I had that experience again. The morning *Dolly!* opened, David Merrick called me up and said, "Get out of bed, jump in a cab, and get down here. You are going to see something that only happens once in a lifetime." When I got to the St. James, there was a line all the way around the block. And there was David Merrick going down the line, serving the people hot coffee. I nearly fainted.

That was an incredible moment. But *Nightcap* was the very first, and there is nothing like that feeling you get the first time. I will remember it always.

Thanks to the rave reviews we continued to pick up, *Nightcap* became *the* cabaret show to see. The society set came down in limousines from uptown, wearing their furs and evening gowns. Everybody got a terrific kick out of jamming themselves into this funky little Village nightspot.

One rainy afternoon, this smart-looking woman came into the club with a handsome escort. Her name was Priscilla Morgan and she was a talent representative. Priscilla became my first agent, and in the years ahead I would never see her without a handsome escort.

Nightcap ran for two years. I kept it fresh by changing the comedy material, which I did by using topics right from the headlines. I also had to keep replacing the cast in those two years. Estelle Parsons, Rita Gardner, and Bobo Lewis all came and went. It was like a stock company. The place was always crowded and I had a nice little percentage of the income.

Finally, I even replaced myself at the piano. It was time for me to go on to something else. *Nightcap* was my first taste of success and it was delicious. Now I was really on my way!

THREE

"Let's Not Waste a Moment"

WELL, IT HAD to happen—I got a bad review. For the first time in my life, I got a slap on the wrist. And wouldn't you know, it had to come from the New York *Times*.

The pain of that first bad notice was horrendous. But it was also an important learning experience, because it taught me that I had inner strength and resources that I never knew about. Thanks to that first negative notice, I discovered that I was not such a fragile little person after all. I was tough enough to get up the next morning, walk back into the theater, and get on with my life.

The year was 1960 and the show was *Parade,* which came about when my friend Larry Kasha decided that he wanted to be a producer. Larry was this young, brash kid about my own age who was just getting started in the theater the way I was. After Larry saw my 1958 show *Nightcap,* he came to me all excited and said, "Jerry, we have to get this show out of the nightclub and into a theater. Let's get a big-name star, do some scenery and some real costumes, and book it into an off-Broadway theater. I'll raise the money. I can do it."

He didn't get an argument from me. I wrote more material and got a sketch writer to help me expand the show into a real theater piece. We kept Charles Nelson Reilly, of course, because his quirky, quick-witted humor had the audience in stitches. We hired another comedy star, Dody Goodman, who was very big as the zany comedienne on "The Jack Paar Show." Dody's outrageous sense of humor was just right for the show, and when *Parade* opened at the Players Theater on MacDougal Street everyone loved it—except the *Times* critic, who called it "sophomoric."

I was personally devastated, but I forced myself to march into that theater the next day to cheer up my little group. That was my job, because I was their director, their composer and lyricist, even their piano player. I was only in my twenties, but I was their father figure.

Walking into that theater was one of the hardest things I have ever done in my life. I don't know where I got the courage, but I went in there with a big smile and told them how wonderful they were, how proud of them I was.

"Look," I said, "we have to put this in perspective. Six good reviews out of seven is not so bad. And the main thing is that the *audience* loves you. When you hear that laughter, when you see people walking out of the theater with smiles on their faces and humming a song, you have to know that you have done something wonderful."

We all put our arms around each other, because we had become a little family. Then I went out and started the overture—and the second-night performance was terrific!

I'LL TELL YOU something else about *Parade*. It brought out the true optimist in me. I don't know where I got the guts to go backstage to talk to Charles Nelson Reilly and Dody Goodman and all those kids in *Parade*. I just knew I had to keep my show from falling apart. And in the funny way that these things sometimes turn out, I was right to be optimistic, because a few weeks into the run, something wonderful happened.

ONE NIGHT AFTER the show, this tall, distinguished, elegantly dressed gentleman walked over to the piano while I was still playing the walk-out music to get the audience out the door. He handed me his card and introduced himself as Gerard Oestreicher, this very wealthy and successful real-estate man who was well known around town as someone who was hopelessly in love with musical theater.

Mr. Oestreicher told me that he was looking for a composer for a new musical he had in mind. We made a date for lunch, which I remember as a tasteful but rather grand spread at the Carlton House on Madison Avenue. I was even more impressed when he told me that his new project was going to be a *Broadway* show.

"Do you think you can handle something ethnic?"

That was the first thing he asked me, and I hadn't the foggiest idea what he was getting at.

"I think you are very talented," he told me. "But this musical I'm doing will be set in Israel. Do you think you could do that kind of thing?"

Well, I am sitting in this very elegant restaurant, talking to this very rich businessman who can hire anybody he wants for this job, and I am *not* going to admit that I didn't know the first thing about Israel. So I said right away: "You have come to *exactly* the right person. I grew up in a Jewish home and I had a Jewish mother who taught Hebrew music at the YMHA in Jersey City."

That was all I had to use for a credential—so I used it for all it was worth.

"I am a totally American writer, but I know *all* those Hebrew songs," I told him. "And more important than knowing the music, I grew up with that heritage all around me. I would have absolutely no trouble writing this show."

I talked a good game. And a week later I was on a plane, flying to the Middle East.

I ALSO FOUND myself on this plane with a total stranger—an older man named Don Appell who was the book writer. Don turned out to be very sweet and very easy to work with, but at that time we didn't know each other from Adam. Our producer had put the two of us together and scheduled this trip so that we would be in Israel for the country's thirteenth Independence Day celebration.

So here are these two total strangers sitting next to each other on a plane, flying to the Middle East. Between the two of us, we hadn't the vaguest idea what we were going to do. All we knew was that this rich real-estate man wanted us to come back home with an American musical about the state of Israel.

Don and I had no source material to work from. None. No play, no novel, no idea. What we were given were these vague instructions: "Go. Go to Israel. Go get some ideas. Go fill yourself with Israeli music."

This was actually very interesting to me—at first. But to my horror, I soon found out that there was no such thing as a "musical heritage" for a country that was only thirteen years old.

I nearly panicked, but I talked myself out of it because I just couldn't go back to being a scared little bunny again. I had to rise to the challenge and be a *mensch*. So I just turned very casually to this total stranger and said, "Okay, Don, what are we going to write about?"

Thank God, he had an idea.

"There's a lot of group travel these days," he said. "What do you think about a group of American widows who are taking a tour of Israel? One of them meets a man and . . . well, we can go on from there."

I loved the idea and we started talking about the actresses who could play the widows. The name Molly Picon popped out of both our mouths at the same time. I knew about Molly Picon from my parents, but Don had actually seen all her performances in Yiddish theater pieces and he absolutely adored her.

Don was enchanted with the whole idea of writing for this great star. He said, "I am going to write a part for Molly Picon, and it will be so delicious that she won't be able to turn it down."

And that's about all we had when we got off the plane in Jerusalem.

WE WERE TREATED like royalty in Israel.

Our producer Gerry Oestreicher had very cleverly contacted the Israeli government beforehand, and told them that we were coming to write this very happy and very positive show about their country. The government was thrilled about the whole idea, of course, because Israel still had an image problem in 1960 and the publicity wasn't all that terrific.

We were met at the airport in a limousine, as guests of the government. They put us up in luxury at the King David Hotel and then we were literally *ushered* through the country like visiting princes. The way they rolled out the red carpet in Tel Aviv and Haifa and Jerusalem, you had to be impressed.

But it was the desert that really etched itself in my mind. I couldn't get over how these people had taken this barren part of the world and turned it green and fertile. I remember driving down a road past these lush groves of trees. Rows and rows of strong young trees. And on the other side of the road was the land the way it used to be—miles and miles of endless sand. Seeing that landscape, I felt deep respect for these people who were trying so desperately to make something live and grow in this desert.

But let's face it—we were being given the propaganda tour, and we knew it. They showed us all the wonderful things about Israel, but we weren't allowed to see anything we weren't supposed to see.

After a few days of this, Don turned to me and said, "Jerry, I don't want to spoil your fun—but are you as sick of this as I am?" And I said, "I am *so* glad to hear you say that! I thought it was just me."

So we got our own car and took off. We needed to meet some real people and see what we could see on our own.

We drove to the border cities, where you could get a much different sense of the country. We saw some unrest, and a fierce chauvinism that was pretty unpleasant. We met people who were poor and people who lived in constant fear of being shelled from the other side of the border.

"The children are the only ones who sleep through the night," this one woman told us. "The old ones sleep with their ears open, listening for the shells to come in the middle of the night."

I didn't love everything we saw in Israel, and I wanted to be honest about that. I didn't want this show to be just a patriotic love letter to the state of Israel. Something rubbed me the wrong way about saying how absolutely marvelous everything was in this country, if I could not mention the things I saw that were not so marvelous.

I found a way to show both sides of the story musically in the title song. "Milk and Honey" is what it is—a patriotic anthem.

> "What if the earth is dry and barren
> What if the morning sun is mean to us, for

> This is a state of mind we live in
> We want it green and so it's green to us, for
> When you have wonderful plans for tomorrow
> Somehow even today looks fine, so
> What if it's rock and dust and sand.
> This lovely land is mine."

But what really pleases me about that song is that it also expresses in counterpoint the honest ambivalence that many Israelis have about their country.

The character who expresses this ambivalence is Adi Gluck, the grumbler, the one who is always complaining about the hard life in Israel. This excellent actor named Juki Arkin played the part of Adi, and he gave him just a little edge of cynicism that made him real.

In the title song everyone else glorifies Israel by singing: "This is the land of milk and honey." But Adi sings:

> "The honey's kind of bitter and the milk's a little sour
> Did you know the pebble was the state's official flower
> What about the tensions, political dissensions, and no one ever
>   mentions
> That the scenery is barren and torrid and arid and horrid
> How about the border when the Syrians attack?
> How about the Arab with the rifle in your back?
> How about the water? What there is of it is brine
> But this lovely land is mine."

The show came out a valentine, but I was proud of that gray shadow that made it truthful.

I GOT THE idea for another song the very first day I was in Jerusalem.

Here I was, a Jewish boy from a Jewish home and all that—

41

but a Hebrew scholar I was not. I didn't know a single word of the language.

There was this one word, though, that Don and I must have heard a hundred times that first day. I couldn't figure out what it meant because people would say it as a greeting, they would say it as a goodbye, they would say it to mean so many things. The word was *Shalom*.

So I turned to Don and I said, "You know, you can practically get along in this country if you only knew this one word—and when to say it."

"Shalom" became my first song. I had that song written in my head before I ever got to a piano. There's a lyric in it that gives the song a certain poignancy.

> "And even when you say goodbye
> If your voice has 'I don't want to go' in it
> Say goodbye with a little 'hello' in it.
> And say goodbye with Shalom."

There was something else about that song. It was the first time that I had a collaborator, somebody I could talk to about a song I was writing. It was a very pleasant experience. It was lovely, actually.

When I threw that "Shalom" idea to Don, he threw it right back to me with his own idea. "Let's make the scene a Hebrew lesson between the two middle-aged lovers on their first date," he said.

Once he gave me that suggestion, I saw how the song could help these awkward lovers to get to know each other. It wasn't just a cute song with a nice melody. That song had a point to make in the story and gave the audience a reason to fall in love with these charming characters.

That was a classic example of musical theater collaboration because Don and I found that song together. We worked like that for the whole show. Don was older and more experienced, but he never patronized me and we had an equal and respectful relationship. I loved working with him.

PEOPLE MIGHT THINK that because I write both music and lyrics, I don't like to collaborate. But it's exactly the opposite. I have always loved to collaborate, because I do two people's work, and when you do two people's work, it can be very lonesome.

Kander can say to Ebb, "How do you like this melody?" and Kander can always get some kind of response from Ebb. I have to say, "Jerry, what do you think of this melody?" Then Jerry has to answer, "That's nice," or "Play it again and let me think what I can do with it."

I'm not complaining, because I love writing music and lyrics. But it's still very lonesome.

Then there are composer-lyricists who will say that they like collaborating with a book person, but they dread collaborating with a director. You finally get everything perfect, and then the director comes in and shakes everything up and says: "I don't like this. . . . Change that. . . . Do this over."

I love it. I am actually happiest when I start right off working with a director and a book writer. And then going on to work with the choreographer, the scenic and lighting designers, the whole team.

The team on *Milk and Honey* was perfect for someone who had never done a Broadway show because they were all top professionals I could learn from. Albert Marre was a very respected Broadway director whose elegantly simple style was absolutely right for this show. He was also a real gentleman who never tried to push something past Don and me, so I came to trust his good judgment. Some things I learned just by watching pros like Donald Saddler, the choreographer, do their work. We also had this brilliant choral director, Robert

DeCormier, who did amazing things with the vocal arrangements to give the music a rich sound and an exotic ethnic flavor.

That collaboration, that incredibly tight teamwork, is what the American musical theater is all about—or what it used to be about, anyway. The American musical is not this person or that person running the show. It is a team of people putting all their individual talents together to create one brand-new thing. If it is well done, the way a show like *Oklahoma!* is well done, you can't pick apart the different pieces that each person contributed.

That was the kind of collaboration we had on *Mame* and *La Cage aux Folles,* which were the two greatest experiences I ever had in the theater. And that's why I adored *Milk and Honey,* because it was the first show that started me working with a team of collaborators.

BECAUSE *MILK AND HONEY* was my first Broadway show, every experience was a first for me.

When Don Appell came to my apartment in New York to show me the scene he had written for "Shalom," it was my first scene complete with dialogue, music, and lyrics. I was so thrilled to hear everything come together in that scene, I pushed Don out the door and made him go out for dinner with me to celebrate. The backers' auditions we were doing at Gerry and Irma Oestreicher's gorgeous apartment at the Carlton House were another first. All those rich people had to be *charmed* to put up their money in our show.

It was also my first experience going out of town on a show. We took *Milk and Honey* to the Shubert Theater in New Haven, which in 1961 was a viable place to go for a pre-Broadway tryout. It was summertime, and I remember that we opened on a very hot night. The theater was too warm and I was a nervous wreck pacing in the back of the theater and sweating out the out-of-town opening night—another first.

The show had tremendous energy and everything about the physical production looked fabulous: Howard Bay's stunning sets, Miles White's colorful costumes, and the brilliant choreography by Donald Saddler. By the end of the "Independence Day Hora" the audience was stamping its feet with the music. But I don't think I actually breathed until Molly Picon stopped the show with "Hymn to Hymie." The audience was laughing so hard at the lyrics, they wouldn't let her get on with the scene.

That number was my absolutely first, honest-to-God show-stopper. What a moment!

BUT HERE'S THE most important first about *Milk and Honey*: it was my very first experience hearing an orchestra play my work. Up until that time I had never heard one bar of my music played by anything more elaborate than piano, bass, and drums. The legendary Hershy Kay was our orchestrator, and the first time I heard the sounds of my music coming from a big show orchestra, I wept from the top of the show to the end. It was a tremendous emotional experience.

Because I saw *Milk and Honey* as a great opportunity for me to really show my stuff, I wrote every conceivable kind of song for that show: romantic melodies like "Let's Not Waste a Moment," which is one of my favorite songs; comedy numbers; stirring anthems and folk dances; and a lively hora for the Independence Day celebration scene.

I even wrote my first hotel-room song for *Milk and Honey*. That's a song that you write out of town to get yourself out of some kind of jam. A dreary hotel room in a strange city is not exactly a conducive atmosphere for getting your muse to fly in the window, but I actually enjoy the pressure. It revs me up. You just tell me: "I have to have it by tomorrow afternoon"— and you'll have it.

Some of my favorite songs, in fact, are songs that I wrote in hotel rooms. I wrote a lovely song called "To Be Alone with You," for *Ben Franklin in Paris*, in a hotel room. "So Long, Dearie" was a hotel-room song. Probably my best hotel-room songs are "I Don't Want to Know," from *Dear World* and "Before the Parade Passes By," from *Hello, Dolly!*

The hotel-room song I wrote in New Haven for *Milk and Honey* was "Chin Up, Ladies." The show was in no kind of trouble, but I felt the need for another number for Molly, just because she was so adorable and because the audiences were loving her so much they couldn't get enough of her.

Backstage, we were loving her, too. Once, just before a matinee performance, I caught her with a funny look on her face. Not exactly sad, but distracted, like she had something on her mind. But when she heard her cue it was like this little lightbulb went off inside her, and she was magic.

THE THING THAT people always want to know about the *Milk and Honey* score is how I could have written "Hymn to Hymie" or "Let's Not Waste a Moment," or all those other songs about the intimate feelings of older people, when I was just a kid in my twenties. I didn't even look like I shaved.

Well, for one thing, the central love story was very sweet and innocent. We'd be laughed off the stage today for that story, which was about a woman who was so faithful to her belief in marriage that she wouldn't live with the man she loved until they were both free to marry. But that was a believable story concept in 1961, when our morals were very different than they are today. Audiences were charmed and moved by that love story.

But yes—I *was* a little anxious about writing songs for middle-aged lovers and lonely widows. Emotionally, I was still a child. At that time, I was just finding my own sexuality, and that also made me nervous. I was working with people I didn't know, and I was scared what they would think if they knew about me. I was afraid they might think that a young gay person couldn't write songs for these characters.

I was also concerned because I was not musically trained. For years, I would never talk about this. It was almost a secret. I thought people would treat me with less respect if they knew that I was unschooled.

MILK AND HONEY was the beginning of my musical education. I wrote complicated rhythms and counterpoint and a lot of other technically intricate stuff for that show. I was having the time of my life, but I honestly didn't know what I was doing. I was just using my ear and my instinct.

I knew what I wanted the music to sound like, but I didn't know which instruments made the sounds I wanted. At that point, I didn't even know what a French horn sounded like. Hershy Kay, who was a classical arranger and a learned musician, would sit for hours and instruct me.

My music is *still* a mystery to me. To this day, I don't know how I went to the piano when I was just a little kid and played an F-minor sixth chord. I learned much later what to call that chord, but I still can't explain where it came from.

The real truth is, I don't know how I write—period. I don't know where it comes from and I can't explain to another human being how to do it. So the short answer to the question of how I wrote a Broadway musical with no musical training is: I just did it.

* * *

IN THE SAME way, I wrote for these characters without even thinking about their age. I just did it. One song I wrote was for an older man who falls in love and feels young again. He has just come in from doing heavy work in the fields with all the young men, and he sings:

> "Like a young man
> With a young dream
> You will find me laughing at time
> I will plow the desert in the morning
> With the power of a boy
> Guard the border if I have to
> In the blaze of the sun I can handle a gun like a toy
> I'll make grain grow
> Out of nowhere
> 'Til the gray sand turns into gold
> Like a young man
> Who's young forever
> I swear I'll never grow old."

That was the song that won over Robert Weede when I went to his apartment to play him the score. Bob was an opera singer and he had also done *The Most Happy Fella* on Broadway. So he brought his robust sound and this wonderful vigor to the song.

Bob also had an actor's understanding of the meaning of a song. When he sang his big ballad at the end of Act One, his voice pulsated with a sense of urgency that was absolutely right for a character who didn't want to let a new love slip away from him so late in his life.

> "Let's not waste a moment
> Let's not lose a day

> There's a short forever
> Not too far away
> We don't have to hear the clock remind us
> That there's more than half of life behind us. . . ."

Now that I am that character's age myself—and still thinking and feeling and behaving like a young man—I can see that the sentiments of that song were honest and authentic. But how I knew that back then, I'll never know.

The truth is, I really don't believe that age, or sex or even experience matters that much when you are writing for a character, so long as you can *imagine* yourself to be the person you are writing for. That's how I was able to write "Hymn to Hymie," which is a song for an older woman who talks about the difficulties of living alone after her husband dies.

I wrote that song as a comedy number for Molly Picon, who just ate it up. It had joke after joke about the problems of cooking for one and trying to get a restaurant table for one. The line everyone loved was "How hard it is to make a *tsimmis*"—which is this elaborate stew that Jewish mothers would make in huge batches for their families—"just for one."

The song always got big, big laughs. Sometimes Molly had to do her trademark somersault to break the applause, so we could get on with the show. But it was also a very touching song about being old and being lonely. This widow was remembering all the little things about her husband that used to irritate her, and now these are the very things she misses most.

At this point in my life, I had not yet had a romance of my own, so I had no personal experiences with romantic loss and regret. But I knew what touched me, and I was touched by these images that came into my head of situations that might be terribly lonely for someone who had been happy doing everything as part of a couple.

Many years later, after my own lover died, I saw how true

some of those lines were that I had written thirty-five years ago.

IF EVERYTHING ABOUT *Milk and Honey* was a learning experience, one of the more painful things I had to learn was how to make cuts.

Don Appell was good with the dialogue cuts, but it was up to me to cut this big aria in Act Two that I had written for Mimi Benzell. Mimi had this absolutely exquisite voice and she sang this piece of music beautifully. Musically it was quite intricate, but it was just not the right piece for a musical comedy. The tone was wrong. I knew the song was wrong, but I was still very shaky when I had to cut it from the show—and find a way to tell Mimi.

I made Mimi happy by giving her a reprise of "There's No Reason in the World," a song she loved. There is nothing like the reprise, because it actually *teaches* the audience the song by letting them hear it again.

Very few people know the value of the reprise or how to use it artfully, by changing a word here and there to switch the meaning or broaden the context. Andrew Lloyd Webber understands the technique, and Rodgers and Hammerstein were the masters. I remember how ravishing the melody of "Some Enchanted Evening" sounded to me when I heard it reprised in the second act of *South Pacific*. To me, the reprise is the glue that holds the whole score together.

I PICKED UP so many things working on *Milk and Honey*. I got the shock of my life, standing in the back of the Shubert Theater in New Haven, when I actually *felt* the audience for the first time.

The director, Albert Marre, and I were standing in the back

of the theater, whispering about the little changes that still needed to be done before we got to Broadway, when all of a sudden we felt something different in the air.

We couldn't hear any breathing! It was as if the audience was frozen. There has never been an audience in the world that didn't cough or sneeze or rustle something. But this audience was so absolutely, completely quiet, it sounded like everybody had gone home.

Up on the stage, Tommy Rall had just finished singing "I Will Follow You," which is a very emotional moment in the show. Tommy was playing this young Israeli who adores his American wife. In this song, he realizes how homesick she is, and he promises to leave his own beloved country to make her happy. And when he finishes singing this heartbreaking love song, he leaps off a rock and does the wildest dance you ever saw.

Tommy was the handsomest young man and a wonderful dancer and the audience was absolutely mesmerized. I remember thinking to myself: *This is it.* This is what it sounds like when you have done everything right and your show goes over the top.

From that moment, I started listening hard to the audience and taking notes on every reaction. I still do that faithfully.

David Merrick, who was alternately cruel and kind to me throughout *Hello, Dolly!,* gave me another valuable lesson about the audience.

"Do you want some good advice?" he asked me, when we were in the depths of despair in Detroit. "Go up and sit on a chair in one of the theater boxes. Wait until the show starts, then turn your chair around and watch the audience for the rest of the evening. You will learn more about your show than anything your producer or director can tell you."

It was also David Merrick who made me an absolute maniac about theater temperature. He gave me a lot of brilliant and crazy tips when he was in his rare good moods, and one of them was that you lose your audience when the temperature in a theater goes over seventy degrees. Even in the winter, he always kept the temperature in his theaters down in the sixties.

"What happens if someone complains they're cold?" I asked him. He gave me this wicked smile and said, "I just tell them to clap their hands to keep warm."

NOWADAYS, PEOPLE DO not *start* their musical education on Broadway, the way I did. I was still doing everything by instinct and by ear on *Milk and Honey*. But I was learning, and by the end of my experiences out of town on that show, I felt like a musician.

But nothing—absolutely nothing—could have prepared me for the thrill of my first opening night on Broadway.

FOUR

"Big Time"

WHEN *MILK AND HONEY* opened on Broadway at the Martin Beck Theater on October 10, 1961, opening night was still *opening night*. The critics didn't come in advance to preview performances, the way we do it today. They all came as a group to this one special performance. It was chancey, it was dangerous, it was *horrible*—but that's the way it was done on Broadway in those days. The success or failure of all our work hung on that one performance.

There were many more critics back then, and they were all lined up in the aisle seats of the orchestra, because that was also part of the opening-night ritual. I took one look at that lineup of grim, unsmiling faces and I was terrified.

I ran to the back of the theater, which is where I spend every opening night—pacing. There is a lot of worn-out carpeting in New York theaters thanks to me, because I am a terrible pacer. When I started working on *Hello, Dolly!* with Michael Stewart, I found someone who was even worse than I am about opening nights. Mike never even went to the theater. He would say, "I just can't deal with it, Jerry," and he'd run across the street to some bar.

There's a problem, though, with the Martin Beck Theater.

It doesn't have enough room at the back of the house for pacing. So I had to stand there for the entire show without moving—like I was frozen stiff.

I will always remember the opening night of *Milk and Honey* as the most joyous and the saddest evening of my young life in the theater. The joy I felt was knowing I had written a hit show, but it was also a very bittersweet feeling for me, because my mother couldn't be there.

My mother's mother was in the audience that night, and my mother's sister Belle. So was my father, proud as could be with his second wife, and all my mother's dearest friends. I had invited them all because it was the closest I could come to having my mother there. That whole night, I went up and down on a seesaw of emotion between sadness and euphoria.

In every other way, it was a perfect opening night. The audience laughed and cried and clapped their hands in rhythm with the songs, and when the curtain went down we all ran backstage and had a party in Mimi Benzell's dressing room. There was a more festive affair at the Oestreichers' home and a fancy party at some hotel, but this little backstage celebration was an intimate family affair.

You have to understand that all these people—Molly Picon, Mimi Benzell, Robert Weede—had become like a family to me. Mimi and Bob were our glamorous stars from the Metropolitan Opera Company, and Molly, who was as lovable in person as she was on the stage, was like the mother of us all. I adored them all. They were taking the place of the mother I had lost and the brothers and sisters I had never had. And they adored me.

The feeling of family that comes from working together on a show is something that I never lost over the years. I have always been very close and warm and loving with all my stars. Many of them, like Carol Channing and Angela Lansbury, have become lifelong personal friends.

The moment when the *Milk and Honey* "family" all walked into Sardi's together was very special and truly wonderful. The whole place stood up and applauded. We all sat together as a group, and we were still glued together at our producer Gerry Oestreicher's apartment just before midnight, when the reviews started coming in. The reviews were raves. One or two critics carped about the old-fashioned book, but for the most part they said the show was a lovely experience and the word *melodic* was used a lot to describe my music. The New York *Times* headline read: "All Milk and Honey at the Martin Beck" and *Newsweek* said: "The stage rocks with excitement." It went on and on.

When the last review was read, Gerry Oestreicher came over to me and gave me a big hug and said: "We're a hit." Well, I have heard those words many more times in my life, but there is nothing to compare with hearing them for the very first time.

My most vivid memory of that opening night actually came later, when I walked into my empty apartment and shut the door. It was the middle of the night and everyone else in the show had gone home to their families and loved ones. I was all by myself. I had nobody to talk to. I didn't even have a pet. But I remember standing there and thinking: *"You have a hit show on Broadway!"* It was absolutely the most extraordinary feeling in the world.

THE WHOLE DIRECTION of my professional life changed after *Milk and Honey*—but the changes in my personal life were much more gradual. I have to say that I was not very outgoing sexually and I was not very sure of myself in general social situations. That sense of insecurity continued to plague me through most of my life, long after some of the top theater professionals in the business had become my friends and colleagues.

My relationship with Barbra Streisand, I think, suffered from my sense of insecurity. I was at my most foolish with her, because I was always in awe of her, which was stupid of me. She was delightful and she treated me beautifully. I gave her a gold-and-diamond stickpin for the film opening of *Hello, Dolly!* and she wrote me back the most gracious note. But I never felt comfortable enough to make a friend out of her, and that was a shame. After all, we were both Jewish kids from New York. We could have had a good time together. We could have been pals.

I met Barbra when she started working on the film of *Dolly!* and she asked me to write a new opening number. She had just recorded the "Minute Waltz" and she wanted to open the show with a song like that. "You know how I love to do those fast things," she told me. "Can you write me something I can do at a really fast clip?"

Well, I knew how to write exactly the song she wanted. But when I went to her house to deliver the song, I kept our meeting on a professional level. I wasn't even secure enough socially to invite her out to lunch.

This was a girl who was even younger than I was. When she came to the door to let me in, she was dressed very casually and holding her baby, Jason, who was about six months old, under her arm. What I *should* have said was: "Barbra, let's go to Hamburger Hamlet for lunch—and let's bring Jason."

But that never happened, because even though I was sure of myself as Jerry the composer, I wasn't at all sure of myself as Jerry the person. So I kept my meetings with Barbra very businesslike because I felt more comfortable on that impersonal professional level.

I still wonder what she thought of me. She must have thought that I was cold. If I were meeting Barbra Streisand for the first time today, I would be much more natural and relaxed. But at that time I was doing what I always did in social situations—I was wearing what I call my charming mask.

PEOPLE DON'T KNOW this, but I have worn social masks for most of my life, and being charming was my best form of protection. I always knew how to smile, and when I was very young I actually *learned* how to be charming from my mother and father, who were very charming people, and from their friends.

My parents had this wide circle of sophisticated friends who would gather in each other's homes for these wonderful parties that lasted into the wee hours, with everyone singing and dancing and having fun. Just think of *Mame* and that will give you an idea of the parties I grew up on. On party nights at our house, my mother always allowed me to stay up and spend a half hour or so having grownup conversations with these interesting people.

One of my special favorites was Lil Feinberg, this statuesque lady who was in the fashion business. I remember having long, serious discussions with this very elegant lady who was gracious enough to give a child her close attention. A few years ago, I was walking on Madison Avenue with my friend Carol Dorian, and I ran into Lil Feinberg. The woman must have been up in her seventies, but she was still stunningly coiffed and dressed. And she was still the most utterly charming lady.

I have always stayed in touch with Elsie Bailyn and Lily Sepenuk, two other ladies who were my mother's lifelong friends. Elsie and I speak on the phone every couple of weeks, and I recently made a special trip to Fort Lauderdale just to take Lily out to dinner.

You don't consciously think of these things when you are doing your work, but I wouldn't be surprised if bits and pieces of people like Lil and Elsie and Lily went into the characters I wrote for. And although I didn't realize it when I was a child, these lovely people taught me how to be charming, and it's a good thing, because sometimes I've needed it.

Of all the exciting new adventures that came my way after *Milk and Honey,* one of the happiest was moving from a one-room flat into my first real apartment. That was the beginning of a lifelong interest in architectural design and decorating that eventually turned into a second career for me.

I didn't move very far—just around the corner from 6 East Tenth Street to 3 East Ninth Street—but that apartment became one of my favorite homes. And at last count, I have lived in more than a dozen.

My new apartment was a floor-through with a garden and a fireplace and separate rooms, so I could have a bedroom, a dining room, even an office. I had great fun decorating it. I took off all the doors and made new ones, using new wood that I stained to look like old barn doors. It had a very country feeling and I did the whole apartment in that style: fabrics, furniture, everything. The look was light pine and brick, and I used a very clean, fresh color scheme of beige and white, with royal blue accents. When I was finished, it was really stunning. I was comfortable entertaining friends in that apartment, which also became my private world where I could always retreat.

Without really knowing what I was doing, I was also finding out the kind of person I was. I was becoming a *mensch.*

I didn't do anything really crazy at first. I became a member of ASCAP and used my weekly royalty checks to buy some nice clothes and to pay for fixing up my apartment. Socially, I was spending more time backstage at the Martin Beck, which had become my second home, than gadding about town. But there were certain parties and formal "state" occasions that I really couldn't get out of.

I was nominated for a Tony Award for the score of *Milk and Honey,* so of course I had to show up for that, but not without a whole crowd of friends for moral support. My best friend Carol Dorian stayed close to me, I remember, and some other good friends who were very happy for me.

There was no chance that I would actually win, not against competition like Noël Coward and Richard Rodgers. I am sure that when they announced my name everyone in the theater looked at each other and said: "Who is *that?*" But just being named out loud in such distinguished company was a thrill, and I enjoyed that moment to the hilt.

Looking back over these big events, I can see that I should have enjoyed them more. The truth is, I didn't, because I hadn't completely come out of my shell.

It took me years and years to feel comfortable at these fancy social evenings. I could always rev myself up and get through them, but I was not the life of the party.

Socially, I was just this totally unremarkable person. I was never the aggressive type who could dance into a room and say, "Hi, everybody! Here I am!" I always kept myself off to the side, and if somebody came over and talked to me I was just fine. In fact, I usually ended up using that person as my security blanket for the whole evening.

THEN I DID something brave. Although I had a hit show running on Broadway, I wrote an off-Broadway musical.

The show was called *Madame Aphrodite* and I am sure that very few people have even heard of it. The production was a total failure, the music was never recorded, and the whole thing was swept under the rug very quickly. But in retrospect I think it was brave of me to stretch myself on this material, which was odd and interesting and tough. It was something that appealed to me at the time, and to tell the truth, it still appeals to me today.

The story came from Tad Mosel, this wonderful playwright who had won the Pulitzer Prize for *All the Way Home*. Priscilla Morgan, who was my very first agent and who took me with her to William Morris, used to have these musical evenings at her apartment and invite her clients. They were very sociable get-togethers, and that's where I met Tad. When he showed me this play of his, I was fascinated because it was so different from the kind of thing that I had been doing.

Madame Aphrodite was this dark, almost creepy little parable about an ugly old woman who makes this bogus beauty cream on her kitchen stove and sells it to her neighbors as a kind of revenge for their meanness to her. I have always been drawn to outrageous, larger-than-life female characters, and I could just picture this crazed, bitter old woman in her colorful rags, standing over her stove and stirring her pot of vile ingredients.

Madame hires this nice young man who is a bit of a dreamer as her salesman. He really believes that the cream has magical powers, and that's what he promises this sweet, shy girl who buys the cream. This very plain girl comes to believe that she is turning into a beautiful woman and she attributes her transformation to the miraculous cream. But Madame Aphrodite is touched by the girl's innocence and she admits that the cream is a fake. She tells the girl that it wasn't the beauty cream that changed her from a little mouse that nobody notices into this radiant creature who wins a beauty contest. It was her love for the nice young man.

It was an odd but wonderful fairytale.

The concept of the piece also intrigued me because in an era when musicals were all in bright, happy Technicolor, this show had a dark, magical quality. I wrote a very interesting score, but this was not a bright, happy musical. This was long before the days of *Sweeney Todd*, so this strange little show was well ahead of its time.

Madame Aphrodite opened at the Orpheum Theater with Nancy Andrews as our star. Nancy had played the Broadway lead in *Little Me* and she had a big voice and a big personality, not unlike Merman in some ways. She really put her heart into it, but the show was a dismal failure and lasted only a few performances.

Looking back, I can see that the production really wasn't very well done, and maybe it wasn't the interesting piece that I thought it was at the time. But I can honestly say that I did this project for the right reasons—because I had a very strong affinity for the material and because I felt that it would make me grow as an artist.

The biggest mistake people make in the theater is doing a show for the wrong reasons. They don't really love the material, but they think it will become a commercial hit or they want to be associated with the people involved. These are not good reasons.

I only made that mistake once in my career, when I let Michael Stewart talk me into doing *The Grand Tour*. "Oh, come on," he said, "I'll be your collaborator and you know how we love to work together. The people involved in the show are all darling, and we'll have such a good time."

Well, that may be true, but it's not why you do a Broadway musical. I would rather work on material that I really, really love—like *Dear World* or *Mack and Mabel* or a little show like *Madame Aphrodite*—even if it turns out to be a commercial failure.

HAVING SAID THAT, I now have to admit that my biggest hit and probably my most beloved show—*Hello, Dolly!*—was a horrendous experience. I adored writing that show and it ultimately gave me great pride and satisfaction. But during the whole time that we were out of town, it was nothing but heartache.

I really *hated* working on *Dolly!* out of town, and I have horror stories about that show that would curl your hair. But before all that madness happened, there was the amazing story of how I got the job in the first place.

Milk and Honey was playing to good audiences at the Martin Beck Theater and there were all these spinoffs. Eddie Fisher had recorded "Shalom" and made a big hit with it. The song was playing all over the airwaves and both the album and the songbook were selling very nicely. And of course there was the Tony nomination.

At some point in all this, the playwright Michael Stewart, whom I didn't know at the time, went to see the show and he liked my work. He started touting me to the producer David Merrick, who was looking around for a composer-lyricist who could work with Michael on a new project for Ethel Merman. Michael finally got Merrick to see *Milk and Honey,* and Merrick was sufficiently impressed to call me into his office.

In those days, just the *name* of David Merrick was awesome, so the idea of meeting him made me a nervous wreck. Going up in the elevator, my knees actually buckled. I was a real baby in the business and still very insecure. And of course I had heard all these terrifying stories about what a monster Merrick was.

Well, the first time I laid eyes on the man, I was sure the stories were all true.

People had told me about that famous red office of his, but it still threw me for a loop when I saw it for myself. It was so *absolutely* red. The walls were covered in fire-engine red felt and the wall-to-wall carpeting was the same violent color. Even the furniture was upholstered in this hot, flaming red. It was like an office in hell.

And here was this man in a black suit, glaring at me with

these dark and piercing eyes. Merrick was not a big man, but he really knew how to present himself as the lord of this under-world. He was sitting in this big leather chair behind this magnificent antique desk. It was a powerful piece of furniture—wonderful dark wood, massive in size, a very strong and gutsy piece. He really was an awesome figure in this setting.

Today, we would call that whole business a very shrewd power play. But Merrick did it instinctively, to make everyone feel uncertain and uncomfortable negotiating with him. He loved having the upper hand, the power position. There is no question in the world that this was a very tough man who loved to intimidate people.

It certainly worked on *me,* I'll tell you. I was not prepared for this kind of craziness and I was scared to death of him.

It was probably the shortest meeting in theater history. "I saw your Israeli musical and I think you're very talented," Merrick told me, "but I don't know if you are American enough for this project. This is Thornton Wilder. This is turn-of-the-century New York. This is very *American* material."

Well, I nearly fell over, because there is nobody more American than I am. Here I am, the child of two school teachers, a boy who is totally in love with the American musical theater. I can't think of a more typical American than myself. The man has just seen this Israeli operetta that I wrote, and he thought I was this little Jewish kid who could only write ethnic material.

I tried to explain as nicely as I could that my sound was totally American, and that *Milk and Honey* was a departure for me. But I could see that he was not really buying this. So I got up my courage and I said, "Do you have any material that I could look at, so I can *prove* to you that I am the right person for this project?"

He went to his shelf and took down a first-draft script—it had a flame-red cover to match the rest of the place, of course—and handed it to me.

I took it from him and I said, "Mr. Merrick, today is Friday. Just give me the weekend. If you let me come back on Monday, I promise I'll have something to show you."

Much later, I found out that he admired me for fighting for this show. The whole time I was in that office I was playing Little Jerry Sunshine out of sheer terror, but the minute I became tougher and more aggressive, he started to have some respect for me. He also appreciated that I was willing to audition for the job, even though I had this big Broadway hit running down the block.

The man was cold as ice about it, but at least he gave me a chance. He gave me three days.

THOSE THREE DAYS were the turning point of my career. I was still living in my one-room walkup at 6 East Tenth Street, so I made a quick trip to the market before I went home. I bought plenty of candy bars because to this day, whenever I want to treat myself for writing a good line or a pretty melody, I shove a piece of candy in my mouth.

Then I went upstairs to my apartment and locked myself in.

I called my father and I said, "Don't anybody talk to me for three days. I have to do this important work." I phoned Carol Dorian and all my close friends and I said, "Please let me be alone for the weekend. I have all this work to do."

Then I sat down to read the treatment by Michael Stewart. It was one of those mimeographed scripts with a thick cover and the title stamped in gold: *Matchmaker Draft #1*. That script is still in my possession. It is one of my true treasures.

I read the script and I read it again and I read it a third time. I started making notes in the margins. Then I went to work.

I wrote "Put On Your Sunday Clothes," word for word and note by note, exactly the way it is in the show. I never changed a thing. The next thing I wrote was the opening number—the whole sequence of "I Put My Hand In" and "Call On Dolly"—and then "Dancing," which is one of my favorite songs from the show. That melody still knocks me out.

The fourth song I wrote was a period piece for Mrs. Molloy, about her departed husband. The first line of it was "I still love the love that first I loved when first in love I fell," and it really did sound like an old English ballad. I eventually replaced that number with "Ribbons Down My Back," but it was a very sweet little song. I think of it as the "forgotten" song from *Dolly!*

I produced those four songs in two days of the wildest, most intensive writing binge of my life. I was like a crazed person, pacing up and down in the middle of the night, scribbling down lyrics and popping candy in my mouth. But I was young, I was full of energy, and I wanted this happy, brightly colored American musical more than anything in the world.

I was like those kids in *A Chorus Line*—I was determined to get this job. There was a new aggressiveness in me, this desperate need to prove something about myself. I *killed* myself for this job.

ON SUNDAY AFTERNOON, I called up Alice Borden, the girl from Stissing Lake. She had acted in all those summer shows I produced at camp, so I asked her to do me this tremendous favor and learn all this material I had written. "Sunday Clothes" needed two voices, and two of the other songs had to be sung simultaneously. It was a fistful of material to learn and we worked on it all Sunday and Sunday night until about 2 A.M.

The next morning, we showed up at David Merrick's office at 11:30 A.M. It was another scene from a Judy Garland and Mickey Rooney MGM musical. This scary man and these two eager, bright-eyed kids. Then Michael Stewart arrived and was introduced to me as the author, which made me all the more nervous.

I said, "Mr. Merrick, I would like to present you with four songs." He did not look happy. He just glared at me from behind that desk as if I were trying to pull some trick on him, because nobody could write four songs in three days. He probably thought I was going to play him some old material. All he said was: "Well, go ahead."

I wasn't presumptuous. I didn't say, "This is the opening number." I said, "This is my *idea* for an opening number." And then I did "I Put My Hand In" the way I wrote it originally, with Alice coming in on the counterpoint. Michael Stewart applauded and Mr. Merrick actually said "Very good."

Then I started tapping out the rhythm of a train and I did the whole sequence of "Put On Your Sunday Clothes" with Alice belting it out with me. They *both* applauded at the end of that one. After playing the ballad, which charmed them, I ended with the whole "Dancing" sequence.

By this time they were both speechless. But before they could say anything, I hit them with that old trick I had learned when I was eighteen years old—I played pieces of all four songs so they could hear them again.

I had gotten good mileage out of the reprise in *Milk and Honey*. When you hear a song once, and then you hear those same notes again a few minutes later, the song settles itself in your ear.

So I played the songs again.

When I finished, David Merrick stood up from behind his big desk and said, "Kid, the show is yours."

FIVE

"A Damned Exasperating Woman"

ON MY TOMBSTONE they are going to say: "He Wrote *Hello, Dolly!*" That's it—that's all people are going to say about me. Most people won't even know that the *Dolly!* period was the most difficult time of my life.

You'd think I would be happy and proud of having written one of the most beloved musicals in theater history. But the truth is, it took me thirty years before I could feel absolute joy and pleasure in having written *Hello, Dolly!*

The closest I came to feeling really happy about *Dolly!* was when I supervised the show for the Houston Grand Opera in 1978. But it wasn't until Carol Channing took the show out on tour in 1994 for its thirtieth anniversary that all the old wounds had healed.

It was such a triumph. Audiences fell in love with *Dolly!* all over again. Even the critics went crazy over the production. They called it "fresh" and "exuberant" and "irresistible." The personal notices I got would make any composer ecstatic. "How brilliantly Herman's great songs embody Wilder's philosophy," one critic wrote. "Rarely has a musical's score so unswervingly served its theme—the characters' reaching out for life." *Time* magazine said that "Jerry Herman's infectious, toe-tapping score remains among the most melodious ever written for a musical."

It was a total triumph, but it had taken me years and years before I could completely enjoy it.

WHENEVER I THINK about *Dolly!*, I picture myself struggling to hold my own in my first meeting with Gower Champion the director, Michael Stewart the book writer, and David Merrick the producer from hell. It was like being tossed into a pool of show-business sharks.

These were very powerful and sophisticated theater people and very tough guys. David, Gower, and Mike all knew and liked each other, and they had already had one Broadway success together with a show called *Carnival.*

I was the new kid in town. I was young and inexperienced, unsure of myself professionally, and uncertain about expressing myself. But as the composer and lyricist on this show, I was doing two people's jobs. It was up to me to stick up for my own ideas, because I had no partner to help me do it.

The first thing I had to learn was how to protect my work. Then, when the show got in trouble out of town and David Merrick pounced on me and made me his whipping boy, I really had to fight for my life. The whole experience forced me to grow up. In that sense it was good for me—but still, so very painful.

IN THE BEGINNING, though, everything was just peachy.

Mike Stewart and I had a lovely rapport, right from the start. After *Dolly!*, we went on to write two more shows together, *Mack and Mabel* and *The Grand Tour,* and we became like brothers. We not only liked each other, we also understood one another's foibles—which was a good thing, because Mike had a very abrasive side to him. There were times when he would really fly off the handle.

I remember when we were out of town with *Dolly!* and David Merrick was on one of his rampages. Mike and I were riding down in the hotel elevator with Merrick, who was blasting away at Mike because he wouldn't change some scene or another. I was cowering in the corner, trying to shrink myself into an invisible person, because this dogfight had nothing to do with me.

But Mike was not giving in to Merrick. He raged right back at him. Merrick had this habit of locking his jaw whenever he was angry, and hissing at you through his clenched teeth like a snake. That's what he did with Mike.

"You're nothing but a hack," Merrick snapped at him. "I don't know why I go on working with somebody who's such a *hack.*"

Now, there is no worse insult to a writer than calling him a hack, especially coming from someone who is supposed to be a good friend. Mike went crazy. By the time the elevator got to the lobby, they were both red in the face from yelling and screaming.

I swear they didn't speak to each other for two weeks.

That was a side of himself that Michael Stewart never showed me, thank God. To me, Mike was not only a talented collaborator, but also my loyal and supportive partner. He was very important to me, and now that he is gone I miss him terribly. But oh, boy, when Mike got mad he had the temper of the seven hounds of hell!

THE WRITING ON *Dolly!* went very easily in the beginning because I had this great character to write for, as well as the lyrical and colorful background of New York in the 1890s.

It was David Merrick's dream all along that Ethel Merman would play Dolly Levi, and the day finally arrived when he thought the score was ready to be played for her. Mike Stewart and I were sitting in his office when he made the telephone call.

The conversation went something like this: "Hi, Ethel, this is David. I have a wonderful new show for you and I'd love to make an appointment for you to hear it." After he said this, there was a long, looooong silence while Ethel talked and talked and went on talking. When David finally got a chance to get a word in edgewise, all he said was: "You're sure, Ethel? You're really sure about that? Okay. Thanks. Goodbye."

He turned to us and said that Ethel Merman didn't even want to *hear* a new score. "I have spent my entire life in a dressing room, and I have had it with that life," she told him. "I want to be free. I want to have some fun. I just want to be able to go to dinner parties at eight o'clock at night, like everybody else does, instead of always eating in the middle of the night."

Well, I could certainly understand her feelings, but we were all absolutely devastated.

Then Gower came up with the idea of casting Carol Channing, this young comedienne he had directed in her first revue, *Lend an Ear*. I actually saw that show. My father and mother had taken me and we thought she was so funny in her big number, which was something called "The Gladiola Girl." Gower said she would be absolutely marvelous as Dolly.

So we all piled into a car and went out to this little theater in New Jersey where Carol was performing in George Bernard Shaw's play, *The Millionairess*. I could see exactly what Gower was getting at, because this woman was remarkable—a bigger-than-life character and a truly gifted comic. We were all instantly enchanted by her. A week later, she was in my apartment learning the score.

The very first thing she said to me was, "I hope this won't upset you, Mr. Herman, because a composer usually hears his songs being sung in a certain way. But you know, I sing lower than the men in your show."

Carol wasn't kidding. She actually sings in male baritone keys that are several tones lower than any of the keys I have written for other ladies to sing in. So what I did was tailor the score for her voice.

I had Ethel Merman on the brain when I was writing the opening number, so it had a very wide range—an octave and five notes. The song suited Carol, but the range didn't. So right there at the piano we found her true keys and I consolidated the range of that song, changing a few notes here and there to make her comfortable.

I was amazed to see how grateful she was for my help. And the moment I heard her sing I said to her, "Miss Channing, this is *exactly* how I hear my songs being sung."

In that moment, she realized that I was there to make her comfortable, and we became instant friends. She knew she had an ally that she could count on.

To ME, THE most wonderful thing about Thornton Wilder's original play, *The Matchmaker*, was its celebration of Dolly Levi's return to the human race. The emotion that really moved me was the idea of this widow coming back to life after a long mourning period, and then finding the courage to do something really important with her life.

You might say that this had something to do with my own extended mourning for my mother—but I really wasn't thinking about that at the time. What I wanted to do with the song "Hello, Dolly!" was to capture the moment when this lady who had locked herself away from life finally gets the guts to put on all her old finery and walk down that staircase to face the world again. That was such a brave, tough thing for her to do. I just loved her for it.

I had absolutely no idea that this song would become such an incredible phenomenon. It was not even my idea to make it the title of the show. We were thinking of just calling it *Dolly*, with the subtitle: "A Damned Exasperating Woman." I had actually written a song called "You're a Damned Exasperating Woman."

The true inspiration for naming the show *Hello, Dolly!* came from Louis Armstrong.

WE WERE STILL working on the show out of town when the Louis Armstrong record came out. That probably sounds peculiar, that a record would come out before opening night, but that's the way it was done in those days, when popular music was still largely based on the American showtune.

Frank Sinatra, Perry Como, and all the top recording artists of the day got their material from Broadway, so they all wanted to hear the new showtunes while the shows were still being written. If you were working on a musical you would cut a demo record to get the songs out before the show went into rehearsal. And if a popular recording artist picked one of your songs, you would hear it all over the radio before your show even opened.

All that changed during the 1970s, for a number of reasons. First of all, Broadway diminished until there were only a couple of new musicals each season to supply the material. At the same time, the public's musical tastes moved away from the showtune to the rock beat, the rap rhythm.

But the biggest reason, I think, is that the singer-songwriter took over from the traditional pop singer. All the Billy Joels and Bruce Springsteens and Carly Simons write and perform their own songs. They don't depend on original Broadway showtunes for their material.

For all these reasons, by the 1970s showtunes were no longer as popular as they were in the '50s and '60s, or in the great heyday of the '30s and '40s. Today you won't hear songs from *Victor/Victoria* on the radio.

I am not saying that you should stop progress and go back to the way things used to be. That's foolish. But it makes me sad that popular music has so little use for showtunes, because that's the music people always loved to sing and dance to. My mother used to call those songs "courtship music," and it hurts me that this music is disappearing.

Even though I accept the fact that demo records are pretty much a thing of the past, it's a tradition that I am personally determined to hold on to. I did a demo of *La Cage aux Folles* in 1983, and I got a Perry Como record of "The Best of Times" and "Song on the Sand." I also got a record by Gloria Gaynor of "I Am What I Am," which became a huge disco hit. And when my next project goes into production, I will definitely make a demo record.

WE WERE OUT of town working on the show, and when you are out of town you are so isolated from the real world, you might as well be on the moon. None of us even knew this Louis Armstrong record existed until someone from my music publishing company in New York got on a plane and showed up at my hotel room in Detroit clutching this little 45 record in his hand and grinning all over the place.

"I am so excited about this record that I had to deliver it to you myself," he told me. "I couldn't even wait to send it through the mail."

All I could say was: "Louis Armstrong? *Louis Armstrong?* That is totally crazy!"

The poor man was *dying* to play me the record, and I have to admit that I was really curious to hear it myself, but there was no equipment at the hotel to play the record on. So we went down to the Fisher Theater, where the company was in the middle of rehearsing a dance number. I asked Gower to call a break so we could hear this new recording.

Gower wasn't all that crazy about being interrupted. But when I told him it was Louis Armstrong doing "Hello, Dolly!" his reaction was just like mine. "Louis Armstrong? *Louis Armstrong?* You have got to be kidding!"

We couldn't begin to imagine what a jazz musician would do with this song. In my mind the whole number felt and sounded very Victorian. It was supposed to be like a scene from *Lillian Russell,* which was this old black-and-white movie starring Alice Faye that had been my real inspiration for the number. Our designers Oliver Smith and Freddie Wittop were working very hard on the right period look—the gaslights and the red velvet staircase and the long white gloves and all that gorgeous, schmaltzy business.

The melody I wrote was also very 1890s. Not the kind of song you tap-dance to, but the kind of song you *sway* to. Like "Shine On, Harvest Moon." So here we were in the thick of all this Victorian atmosphere, when this *jazz* version of our sweet, old-fashioned sing-along song comes blasting over the sound system.

Well, the minute we heard those banjo strums and that rich, gravelly voice, it just took our breath away. Louis Armstrong had not changed a single note or a single word. But by imprinting the song with his own personal style, this incredible musician had made it into a piece of authentic jazz. Our song had taken on a life of its own.

The music publisher started jumping up and down. "That's it!" he said. "That's the title of your show!"

*   *   *

THERE WERE OTHER electrifying backstage moments on *Hello, Dolly!*, but for me the real eye-opener was watching Gower Champion's talent unfold during rehearsal. This man was one of the most inventive stagers in the history of the musical theater, and time after time I watched him pull these wildly original ideas out of thin air.

I remember the exact moment when he came up with the perfect image to let the audience know right at the top of the show that they were at a farce—that it was okay to laugh and have *fun* at this show. We were having a hamburger somewhere near the rehearsal studio when Gower hit us with his idea.

"I'm thinking of opening the show by having this horse pulling Dolly's carriage onstage," he said. "Only I want it to be this goofy-looking horse with a big, silly smile on his face—and with two showgirls hidden inside."

Well, Mike and I thought this was a stroke of genius, because after seeing this funny-looking horse on stage, the audience would accept any kind of zany business. After that, we could make the rest of the show as outrageous as we wanted. Once Gower got his horse, he would be free to do the whole show in wild, wonderful poster colors—bright, happy, not subtle at all—which had been his idea all along.

Gower's giddy cartoon style was also perfect for our star.

We knew we had something quite phenomenal in Carol Channing. It wasn't just her extraordinary personality. It was her sense of timing and her instinct for creating a piece of business. It was the genius of her whole comic style.

I have loved other Dollys, but there were so many original bits and pieces of that show that were pure Carol Channing. It still makes me laugh, the way she can bring the house down with the flip of a napkin.

One of my favorite Carol scenes of all times is when Dolly tries to talk Horace Vandergelder out of meeting Mrs. Molloy. First she manufactures this absurd notion that this pretty young widow had poisoned all her husbands. And after she gets the poor man all worked up, she delivers her devastating last line: "And remember, Mr. Vandergelder, eat . . . out." The way Carol delivered those last two words—taking a long pause and dropping her voice on *out*—was pure inspiration.

To top off the line, Carol had the inspiration to snap her purse shut right in front of his face. David Burns, who was playing Vandergelder, practically jumped out of his skin, and the audience howled.

You have to understand that Carol and her husband Charles Lowe became my best pals during that show. All three of us knew that no matter what happened with this show, we would have a lifetime friendship.

From the moment I laid eyes on Carol, I absolutely fell in love with that delightful woman. We have been through the best of times and the worst of times together, and Carol's unique sense of humor still lifts my spirits.

She is the only star I know who truly loves the discipline of doing eight shows a week. Even twenty-five-year-old kids who are real dynamos will admit that the grueling pace of a Broadway show can knock you out. And here is Carol Channing, seventy-five years old, trouping all over the country again in *Hello, Dolly!* and absolutely thrilled to do it. Trouping is her life.

EVERYBODY INVOLVED WITH *Dolly!* knew that Carol Channing was a natural clown, but that wasn't good enough for Gower. He wanted an entire cast of brilliant clowns.

The only real headache was casting Barnaby. We couldn't find the type of all-American youth who would be exactly right for that Huckleberry Finn role, so there were a lot of replacements before we came up with Jerry Dodge. But we got just what we wanted with Charles Nelson Reilly, who was so naturally funny as Cornelius the clerk that Gower let him use his own offbeat humor to create that character.

That was one of Gower's secret strengths. Like a lot of theatrical geniuses, he had a major ego—but he was secure enough to let his actors contribute their own idiosyncratic style to a character.

Eileen Brennan, who had made a big reputation in *Little Mary Sunshine,* was another inspired clown who brought her own magic to Mrs. Molloy. And David Burns was amazing because he was able to make Mr. Vandergelder irascible and grumpy and endearing and lovable all at the same time. I've seen a lot of Vandergelders who were simply grumpy, but Davey Burns could growl and make you love him because he was harmless—like a little pet tiger.

The cast was so perfect and the designs for the show were so gorgeous that I packed my bags for Detroit convinced that this was going to be another lovely experience, just like *Milk and Honey.* I had these images of us all going to the movies together and enjoying these big, friendly dinners every night.

I was sure we were going to have an absolutely wonderful time.

WELL, IT WAS like getting hit by a bolt of lightning. We got the show up, we previewed, we opened, we thought we had a hit—and the Detroit critics killed us. The mood of the company and the atmosphere of the show changed overnight from happiness to gloom.

No, not even gloom. We were in a state of total *terror* because David Merrick had turned into a wild man. He became crazed with fear that his very costly production was going to flop when it got to New York. The man was in such a state of panic he was incapable of looking at the show's problems rationally.

David Merrick turned into a monster—there is no other word for it—and every one of us came under his wrath.

It was truly a cold day in hell, because it was blizzard weather in Detroit. Winter was horrible in that city. There was ice and snow on the ground, the sky was gray all day, and there was a freezing wind that never let up. I remember huddling in my room at the Park Shelton Hotel, cold and miserable, feeling the entire failure of this show on my shoulders.

That's exactly how David Merrick made me feel, like the whole thing was my fault.

At one point, he turned to me and said, very gruffly, "I am embarrassed to have these songs in my show." This was the very same material, mind you, that I had heard him tout to Ethel Merman as the most wonderful score in the world. Overnight, these very same songs made him sick.

The worst thing is, he said this to me in front of the whole company.

I suppose that I should have been prepared for his cruelty because I had heard plenty of hair-raising stories from close friends of mine in *Subways Are for Sleeping*. They told me how he got on stage after a preview and screamed at the cast the same way he screamed at us.

"I have never been so ashamed in my life," he told them. "I am going to close this awful, embarrassing show."

That was Merrick's technique with people. He made them feel like untalented artists and insignificant people. He really believed that he would get better work out of everybody if he frightened them half to death and made them feel two inches tall.

That technique almost did major damage to our costume designer Freddie Wittop, who went through the tortures of the damned when we were out of town. During one performance in Detroit I found Freddie in tears at the back of the Fisher Theater. When I went over to him and asked him what was wrong, he said that David Merrick had told him that the costumes were ugly and that he was ashamed to have such wretched rags in his beautiful show.

Just then, they started the "Sunday Clothes" number, which opens with a costume parade. As each couple strolled onto the stage in their vibrant costumes, the audience began madly applauding. "Listen to that, Freddie!" I said to him. "Do you hear that applause? Do you know what they are applauding? Not my music, because the song hasn't really started yet. Not the choreography, because the dancers are just walking in rhythm. Not the sets, because there's nothing on stage. They are applauding your gorgeous costumes."

The poor man straightened up and stared at the stage. Then he stared at the audience, which was clapping and cheering. And then he gave me a big hug and went on with his life.

David Merrick's technique of making a person feel small and insignificant almost crushed me, too. That bullying approach was absolutely the worst way to get someone like me to work harder, because it completely inhibited me as an artist. I just closed up inside and thought: "What's the use? That man is never going to like anything I write."

And then the threats started.

First he said he was going to bring in another composer. Then he said he was going to bring in another lyricist. I remember lying awake in bed, listening to the wind rattling the windows, and thinking, "Jerry, you are not going to survive this."

THAT MISERABLE WINTER in Detroit was the only time in my life when I was truly, totally depressed. It got so bad that my best friend Carol Dorian actually sent her husband Bob to rescue me. He was going west on a business trip, and she said to him: "I don't care if it's out of your way. You get on a plane to Detroit and you bring him back home!"

The closest I came to throwing in the towel was when David Merrick started calling in all these composers and lyricists from New York. In the same way that he brought in famous directors like Hal Prince to scare Gower, he brought in famous songwriters to scare me. I know how touchy this can get, because I have spent enough time being a play doctor myself. I wrote a song called "To Be Alone with You" for *Ben Franklin in Paris,* I was called in to look at *Sugar* and *I Do! I Do!,* and I wrote three songs for two dear friends, Tommy Tune and Alex Cohen, to use in *A Day in Hollywood.* So I know how tense these situations can be.

I can't say how Gower or Mike felt about the "help" they were getting from all the outside directors and librettists, but I hated being forced to collaborate. Fortunately for me, that collaborator turned out to be Bob Merrill. Bob and I worked on two songs called "Motherhood" and "Elegance." He was a real gentleman. He truly did not want to be in this awkward position, but he honestly wanted to help, so he gave me the ideas for these two songs and we worked on them together.

Bob wasn't interested in interfering with the show or with my life, and he felt that I was talented enough to do my own work. So after spending some time with me on these two pieces, he left me with material that was deliberately unfinished so I could put my own stamp on it. So I could write lyrics like:

> "All who are well-bred agree
> Minnie Fay has pedigree.
> Exercise your wildest whims tonight
> We are out with Diamond Jims tonight."

When Bob Merrill left town, I thought my nightmare was over.

During this trying period, there was another hotel-room song that I wrote in a flash and which was immediately put into the show. The song was "So Long, Dearie." I remember saying to myself, "Oh, God, Jerry, you better finish that one quickly—before he calls somebody else in."

And then Strouse and Adams arrived.

Charles Strouse and Lee Adams, who were the songwriters on *Bye Bye Birdie,* came to Detroit, met with Gower, wrote a song that Gower rejected, and went back home the next day. To this day I have never heard their song. They were in Detroit only for that one day and their piece was never used.

Strouse and Adams have remained good, supportive friends through all these years. Charlie Strouse even asked me to come in to look at *Nick and Nora*. They got as upset as I did when a book was published that credited them with co-authorship of my song. Charlie Strouse wrote me a handwritten letter that I sent to the author, who promised to correct his error in future editions. But it still makes me crazy when other people perpetuate that author's mistake.

The next day, all those helper elves that David Merrick had called in during his state of hysteria had packed up and gone home. The air cleared and there was this eerie quiet, like a battlefield the day after the battle.

Gower came up to me and said, "Well, it looks like the massacre is finally over and the troops have retreated."

He had this dry sense of humor, so he could laugh things off better than I could. He flashed me that sparkling grin of his and then he said, "Okay, kid—it's up to you."

Well, that was all I needed, the captain of our team *finally* showing that he had some confidence in me. I went straight up to my room and ordered this huge piece of chocolate cake to give me strength. And then I went back to work.

Long before this crisis, Mike Stewart and I had put our heads together and figured out that the real problem with the show was the first-act finale. I had written a song for David Burns called "Penny in My Pocket" that explained how Horace Vandergelder had become half a millionaire. It was a funny song and Davey sang it beautifully, but it was written for the wrong character. By this time, the audience had fallen in love with Dolly Levi. They couldn't get enough of Dolly and they didn't want to listen to some song about how Horace amassed his fortune.

We decided that I would write a whole new closing number—for Dolly.

As far as I am concerned, "Before the Parade Passes By" was the number that saved *Hello, Dolly!*—along with my life and my sanity and my whole future career in the theater. It was the song that finished laying the foundation of the show, because it cemented the weak middle section. And because that song was such an honest emotional moment for Dolly Levi, it deepened her whole character.

To me, that will always be the hotel-room song of all time. Whenever I hear it played, on a taxicab radio or in some supper club, I still get this little thrill.

I wrote "Before the Parade Passes By" in the middle of the night. It is *always* the middle of the night when you are writing a hotel-room song, but this was literally the dead of night. I was feeding myself pieces of this gooey cake and playing that horrible hotel piano very softly, because I didn't want the house detective at my door.

The song I had to write was for that triumphant moment when Dolly resolves to rejoin the human race. I had my image of a parade of happy people, and I could feel the heart-thumping rhythm of a marching band. I could see this woman standing alone on the sidelines, tapping her foot and trying to get up the courage to join the crowd—but wondering if maybe it was too late.

Before I knew it, the song was pouring out.

"Before the Parade Passes By" is not only the heart and soul of *Dolly!*, it is also a metaphor for all of us who reach a certain age and decide that it's all over for us. This song says: "There *are* second chances at life—so take it!"

That dark night in Detroit, when I was sitting in my pajamas writing that song, I could see the longing in that woman's eyes. I could see her clench her fist and make her mind up to get back into life.

It seems so strange to me that I wrote that song at the age of thirty-two, because here I am at that stage of my life right now. I could lock myself up in my beautiful house for the rest of my life and just ignore the parade. I could be that person standing all alone, watching the rest of the world dance by.

But I wrote those words, and they might be the most important words I ever wrote:

> "With the rest of them
> With the best of them
> I can hold my head up high
> For I've got a goal again
> I've got a drive again
> I'm gonna feel my heart coming alive again
> Before the parade passes by."

I *wrote* that. So how could I, of all people, not listen to those words today? Whenever I'm having a tough time, I can always say to myself: "If you pulled *that* off, kid, whatever you have to do today, you can do!"

ANYWAY, BACK IN Detroit it was around two o'clock in the morning.

I was exhausted, but I was also so excited that I had to call up Carol to tell her that I had written her song. Once she woke up and could understand what I was saying, she got so excited herself that she came straight down to my room—in her pajamas and bathrobe.

At first, we just sat side by side at the piano, singing very, very softly. But then Carol said, "The heck with this!"

She went right to the phone and she called up Gower. It was about three A.M. by now, but how mad could he get? She was his star, and when she said, "Darling, I'm soooo sorry to wake you up, but we just can't wait until tomorrow morning," what could he do? He said, "Just give me a minute to throw on a bathrobe and I'll be right down."

By this time the hotel detective must have thought that there was something *really* illicit going on, because it was still hours before dawn and now another person in a bathrobe was sneaking down the hall and into this room.

When I opened the door, I took a deep breath and said, "Gower, I've done it."

I sang the song first. Then I said, "You've really got to hear it in Carol's key." And then Carol—bless her—stood up and belted it out at the top of her lungs. We didn't care if we woke up the whole hotel.

I could see that the great Gower Champion was flabbergasted. And here's how I knew that he was also thrilled out of his mind: he started running around the room. Actually *running*.

Then he started thinking out loud and his creative mind could not stop. "I'm going to put a man in a barrel in the parade. . . . I'll stage the whole march on a ramp. . . . I want a fireman. . . . I want an opera singer! . . . Freddie can do reds and pinks and purples—and polkadots. . . ."

At which point he jumped up on the sofa and yelled: *"I am going to bring back the horse!"*

SIX

"Time Heals Everything"

I KNEW MY misery was over when David Merrick put his arm around me and patted me on the back. And I give myself a lot of credit for not cringing.

That reconciliation, or whatever you want to call it, was all due to Gower, who was up at dawn the next morning and running like a dynamo. He insisted that Merrick go right up to my room to listen to the new tune. And he made it absolutely clear that no matter what Merrick or anyone else thought about it, "Before the Parade Passes By" was going into the show.

So what could Merrick do? He patted me on the back and went back to treating me like his little protegé, his pet discovery.

As far as the show itself was concerned, the really fascinating thing about the new number was how Gower switched into high gear to get it designed, orchestrated, staged, rehearsed, and into the show. He called all the designers and made them jump on a plane to get down to Detroit in two hours. He grabbed the cast before they had finished breakfast and had them up on the stage learning their parts.

We were about a week from going into the National Theater in Washington, and we had no time to fool around.

Gower put everyone on overtime. Oliver had to fake it with a new backdrop. Freddie had people sewing costumes in the middle of the night for the next five days. It was an absolute madhouse.

It was also the most joyous time you can imagine. We really were working like a team again and everybody trusted everybody. The ideas for that number came from everyone—including David Merrick. I think David learned something about collaboration on *Dolly!,* because on his later shows he *listened* to people before making decisions. In fact, we came to respect and admire each other.

That's another thing that has changed about the theater. Instead of one or two producers who know the business and call the shots, you have eight or ten inexperienced producers running around, every one of them with an uninformed opinion. That makes a big difference in the way the work gets done and in the way decisions are made.

I'm used to working with a strong director who can carry his weight with a strong producer, and I'm used to being on a creative team that can work with a strong director. To me, the ideal collaborative director is someone like Gene Saks, who did *Mame,* and Arthur Laurents, who was the director of *La Cage aux Folles.* They were always the boss, but they made their creative people feel as if they were part of the decision making and that their ideas were important.

Nowadays, a producer can't make a decision until he has a meeting or a conference call with seventeen other nervous producers. With shows costing $8 million and more, the economics today are so perilous that everyone goes into the project petrified. That pressure is passed on to the creative team.

The only intelligent way to do a new musical is with a collaborative team who understand and respect each other's work and who know how to *give* to each other. But the teamwork can break down when the production is under that kind of economic pressure. When the stakes are that high, you can't sit around a table as equals, calmly discussing what to do about that problem spot in Act Two.

What happens is, one powerhouse person tends to take over and make all the decisions. It isn't necessarily the director, either. It can be the star or the author, or whoever the producers think has what they call "the muscle."

THE WORK WE did on "Before the Parade Passes By" was true collaboration. I was running around like a crazed person, working with Phil Lang on the orchestrations and with Peter Howard on the vocal arrangements, teaching the song to the chorus, playing rehearsal piano. I was also working closely with Carol to get the emotional delicacy of the opening moment. It was my job to help her understand that the beginning of this song is not a march but a tender and reflective moment.

After putting in the new number for one performance in Detroit, we opened in Washington with our hearts in our mouths. The opening of the show went fabulously. Then came the big moment. I swear I stopped breathing.

Carol did her opening speech with real tenderness. The music came in very quietly and grew in intensity, and when I heard that little snare drum start on the second eighth, and then the oboes joining in, I could feel the hair on my arms standing straight up.

The number was perfect! The house went wild and stopped the show. That told us we had a tremendous hit. For me, that number was also a personal triumph because it had been written under such horrendous circumstances.

That's what makes "Before the Parade Passes By" so important to me. It was a total vindication of my work after my professional humiliation by David Merrick. After that excruciating embarrassment, I was never so determined in my life to write a song and to write it perfectly. It was my way of saying: "I am going to show these idiots that they don't have to call anybody in to do my work. I can do my work myself."

I can say that everything changed after that opening night in Washington. Gower and David took me out to dinner and made me feel like a hero. We were a team again and I was the quarterback the cheerleaders were carrying on their shoulders.

That had been my baptism under fire. From that moment, they treated me with respect. The entire world treated me with respect.

HERE'S SOMETHING I bet nobody remembers about *Hello, Dolly!* We opened in New York after playing only two preview performances. Nobody would do that today if you put a gun to their temple. They would say, "Go ahead, pull the trigger. I will not open my show without previews."

Dolly! didn't need more than those two performances, which were just for technical adjustments anyway. The show had been frozen in Washington after two weeks, which is the time it takes for a new number to hit its stride. And if you want to see me take out *my* gun, just try to get me to change anything during the last week! That makes me crazy!

I have learned the hard way that nothing makes a show go smoother than repetition of the material. Any director who wants to make changes that close to opening is a fool. If you have a better idea—tough. It's too late.

I was my usual basket case for the Broadway opening of *Hello, Dolly!* but Michael Stewart was even worse. Mike stood at the back of the St. James Theater, where I was already pacing up and down, until the curtain went up. But once he saw

With Mom and Dad, New Year's 1935.

My mother, Ruth Herman, and me.

Me at 16.

Ruth Herman at a
flapper costume party.

Me in 1963.
(Photo: Herman Miller)

Here I am in 1965, working on *Dolly!*

Carol Channing and David Burns in the
original 1964 production of *Hello, Dolly!*
(Photo: Friedman-Ables)

Carol Channing as Dolly Levi. *(Photo: Joan Marcus)*

David Merrick being honored by the
Juvenile Diabetes Foundation, with Carol and me.
(*Photo: T. L. Boston*)

Carol and me
in 1963, during
Dolly! rehearsals.

Pearl Bailey
became our Dolly
in 1967.

Barbra Streisand as Dolly in the 1969 movie version.
(*Courtesy Edwin H. Morris & Company*)

Backstage with Ethel Merman in 1970,
the night she opened in *Hello, Dolly!*
(*Photo: Paul Schumach*)

With Ethel Merman and the cast, the night that *Hello Dolly!*
became the longest-running show on Broadway.

Carol Channing and me at the Colonial Theater in Boston,
with the 1978 Houston Grand Opera Company revival of *Dolly!*

Clowning around on the first day of rehearsals with
Angela, Jerome Lawrence, and Robert E. Lee,
and our *Mame* director Gene Saks.
(*Courtesy of Friedman-Abeles Photographers*)

Angela in the title song.

Angela Lansbury in "It's Today" from *Mame*.

At Sardi's in 1966 for the opening night party of *Mame* with Angela and our authors, Jerome Lawrence and Robert E. Lee. (*Courtesy Ken Regan*)

With Angela and Carol.

I love Lucy.

Lucille Ball as Mame in the 1974 movie. (*Warner Bros.*)

The Hollywood version of the title song of *Mame*.
(*Warner Bros.*)

Me in the hospital in 1966 with Eydie Gormé and her
Grammy award for "If He Walked Into My Life."

With my collaborator,
Michael Stewart.
(*Photo: Martha Swope*)

Ann Miller
and me.

With Jule Stein, Hal David, Ginger Rogers,
Ethel Merman, and Lucille Ball.

Angela Lansbury in *Dear World*, 1969.

that the show was actually going to go on, he couldn't bear to watch. He spent the whole opening in a little bar across the street from the theater.

People must have seen me, all dressed up in my tux, with my hands clenched behind my back, walking back and forth like a demented person. But I really couldn't talk to anyone, not even to my loved ones who were all there. My father came with his wife, Edna, and my grandmother and all my mother's friends were there. Maybe the proudest person in the whole audience was my Aunt Belle.

It should have been a joyous occasion for me, but it wasn't. Not really. I had been too badly scarred by the whole experience. I *still* am. And on the opening night of *Dolly!* that scar was still raw.

I'M SURE I wasn't the only one in the house with a private sadness, but we all got caught up in the magic of that performance, which went flawlessly.

Carol Channing reached out for the audience and pulled them in like a magnet. They were mesmerized by her. She had the good sense not to go overboard. That's one of the scary things about opening nights, when people can go over the top and change their performances. Carol was right on her mark. Perfect.

The whole show was dazzling.

The cartoon style that Gower created totally charmed the audience. They laughed at the gaudiness of it all. They loved the bright colors and the gorgeous costumes— and the sets! This was before the big fad of falling chandeliers and helicopters and gigantic turntables. This was when sets were sets, and Oliver Smith's sets were an enchantment, transporting the audience back to the era of gaslights and gilt.

The orchestrations gave the music this wonderful fresh sound, and I give Phil Lang full credit for that.

Philip Lang was my most treasured collaborator because he understood my style and he always knew what I wanted to get across. When we were doing the orchestrations for *Dolly!* I told him that I wanted the last chorus of "Put On Your Sunday Clothes" to sound like a train was pulling right into the St. James Theater.

I sat down at the piano and started to show him. He put up his hand to stop me, and said: "I'm with you. I know exactly what you want. I love it. Trust me."

Whenever Phil Lang said, "Trust me," I knew he understood exactly what I wanted and would give it to me.

Well, the sound of *Hello, Dolly!* was *exactly* what I wanted. I had tried very consciously to make the songs sound like period songs, and it was such a joy to hear that 1890s sound coming from the stage.

In "Sunday Clothes," it's the rhythms that make you feel like you are strolling a New York street in the 1890s. "Dancing" has this graceful waltz step that people in that era could have danced to. And the title song sounds just like a party song that a group of people might have sung around a piano at the turn of the century.

I had great fun working on that sound. I got the same kind of kick trying to sound French in *La Cage*. That's exciting. What I like to do least is write a contemporary sound, because it doesn't give me the challenge—or the fun.

I guess what I really am is a musical playwright. I try to become the playwright in musical terms and write a song that truly expresses and expands the character. For Dolly Levi's songs, the main thing that I kept in my head was her garrulousness. If you look at a song like "I Put My Hand In," you'll notice that Dolly always talks in long speeches, rather than sentences. That woman never shuts up!

NOBODY IN THAT first-night audience at the St. James *wanted* Dolly to shut up. They were singing and laughing and swaying and clapping. That was one happy audience.

Everything after that is a blur for me.

I was whisked out of the theater by my friends the Dorians to go to this festive opening night party that David Merrick had arranged at Delmonico's. David said the party *had* to be at Delmonico's, which was this big hotel with a giant ballroom, because I mention the old Delmonico's in the lyric of "Sunday Clothes":

> "Beneath your bowler brim the world's a simple song
> A lovely lilt that makes you tilt your nose
> We'll see the shows at Delmonico's
> And we'll close the town in a whirl
> And we won't come home until we've kissed a girl. . . ."

At Delmonico's, people were dancing to "It Only Takes a Moment" when I walked in with my little entourage. I remember Gower running over every few minutes and grabbing my arm. "We'll know soon," he kept saying. "The reviews will be out pretty soon, and then we'll know."

Gower also made a point of saying, "You've been a brick through this whole thing, and I am very proud of you." That meant a lot to me, because Gower knew I had been through hell. He had put me through a lot of it himself.

Marge Champion did the sweetest thing. In the middle of all this hysteria, she came over and put her arm around me, and very quietly said, "Has anyone ever told you what a beautiful score you've written?" Because it came at a time when my emotions were so unsteady, I was overwhelmed by the kindness of that gesture.

Around midnight, David Merrick got up on the stage and went over to the microphone. "The first review has come in, and I would like to read it," he told the crowd. "It is by Walter Kerr of the *Herald-Tribune.*"

The whole place froze. My first thought was, "Oh, my God! He is going to read this review *out loud,* to the entire world, and it is going to say something horrible."

Well, of course it turned out to be the most ecstatic review a critic has ever written for a musical. Walter Kerr had this incredible gift for sharing his love of the theater with his readers. When he loved a show, he would really go into raptures. Nobody wrote a rave like Walter Kerr—and Walter Kerr had written us a rave.

"The musical numbers are solid gold brass," he said. "Jerry Herman has torn up a hurdy gurdy and scattered its tinkling waltzes and mellow quartets and tipsy polkas all over Union Square."

That review alone would have made the show a hit, but six more raves came in, one after another. Gower got up on the stage with Mr. Merrick and they took turns reading them. Everybody in the ballroom was going crazy.

But here is the one thing that I really remember through all this blur: Michael Stewart running across the room. He didn't run to his mother, or to his closest friend. He made a beeline for me, his collaborator. He literally ran across the room, yelling, "Jerry! Jerry! Jerry, *we're rich!*"

Then he put his arms around me and started to cry.

That scene of Mike Stewart laughing and crying and yelling "Jerry, we're rich!" is still so vivid in my mind. More than anything else, it made me begin to comprehend what had happened to me.

That's when the enormity of it all really hit me. *Hello, Dolly!*

was not just a hit, like *Milk and Honey* was a hit. This was a big, huge, once-in-a-lifetime hit.

At that moment, I realized that my life had changed forever.

WHAT DOES SOMEONE do when their life changes forever?

The first thing I did was to buy a couple of suits at Paul Stuart. The next thing I did was to buy Edward Albee's house.

Edward Albee's house was a real house, a beautiful townhouse at 50 West Tenth Street, between Fifth and Sixth avenues in Greenwich Village. My little apartment at 6 East Tenth Street had been my first home of my own, but this new place was my first *house*—the first of my twenty-seven houses that I would buy, decorate, and live in happily throughout my life.

Albee's townhouse was actually a fabulous old firehouse that had been converted into a private home by the great stage actor Maurice Evans. It's a two-story house made out of white brick, with front doors that really catch your eye because the wood is so rich and lustrous. Those doors were so gorgeous that I bought a big lantern to hang outside and show them off. It was a charming, unusual place, and it let me stay in the Village, where I felt most comfortable.

But I don't mean that my life changed because I bought a house and two suits. My life changed because I suddenly became a known commodity.

Overnight, I joined the ranks of theater people I held in awe—artists I *still* hold in awe. I was constantly giving interviews and making public appearances. People treated me differently, even people in the street. Strangers would come up and shake my hand.

That kind of heady experience can make you very egotistical and pompous. But that didn't really happen to me because I was such a shy, scared kid before it happened. All the attention just gave me the self-confidence to be a normal person. I could go to a party and have a nice conversation instead of hiding under the piano bench. I could go on a radio program and chat with the other people instead of just sitting there in agony.

During this time in my life I also became more comfortable with my sexuality. I began dating and feeling good about who and what I was. I was an attractive young man and very much in demand, and I had more dates than Palm Springs.

Success did not turn me into a celebrity monster. It was *good* for me, because it helped me to reach a stage that I should have reached five or six years earlier. My success made it possible for me to grow up—finally.

I LOVED REMODELING Edward Albee's firehouse, because it let me express who I was.

Edward sold me his house, which is a landmark building, because he wanted to move to Montauk. It was a wonderful, eccentric house, not a traditional house in any way. That was just fine with me, because I am not a traditional man in any way.

It was only two stories plus a huge basement where they originally kept the fire engines. At one point I actually stored the scenery from *Mack and Mabel* down there. The architecture was beautiful, but everything was kind of upside-down, with the living room on the top floor.

Edward had done the house in a dark style that suited him very well. He had closed the skylight off completely and put these heavy drapes on the windows. There were some beautiful things in that dark living room and it was all very handsome. It just wasn't very happy. George and Martha from *Who's Afraid of Virginia Woolf?* could have lived in that house.

It was all too dark and stifling for me. When I started to

redecorate I felt like I was playing a scene with Miss Haversham in *Great Expectations*. I ran around tearing the drapes down and letting the light in. I am a skylight freak, so I opened up the top of the roof, which was the most exciting architectural feature in the whole house, and designed and installed a copper skylight with etched glass. It was breathtaking, and it made the living room the sunniest, happiest room you ever saw.

I opened up this tremendous space on the first floor by ripping out four or five tiny rooms in the back. That became a dining room that ran the whole width of the house. My memories of the dinner parties I had in that room are absolutely golden.

I also did major work upstairs to design a bedroom that suited me. It was a bright room, because I put in a picture window that faced the terrace. It was a happy room, done in this cheerful color scheme of blue and white. Because I am also a bathroom freak, I eliminated another upstairs room to create this spectacular bathroom with a circular sunken tub. That became the most photographed room in the house.

The renovations took about three months. When the house was finished a lady from *House Beautiful* called up and asked if the editors could come and see what I had done. They took one look at the place and ran a magnificent eight-page, full-color article on my architectural designs.

THAT ARTICLE ESTABLISHED my credentials as a designer. It was the beginning of my second career in architecture and decorating.

My only formal study was that one year at the Parsons School of Design, which is what I call a dangerous amount of knowledge. It wasn't enough so that I really knew what I was doing, but it gave me enough of a background to mix with my natural flair and instinct. The rest I learned by experimenting on my own houses.

It takes a good eye for space to get into architectural design. You have to be able to look at a wreck of a building and be able to say: If I move this and tear down that, and then add a skylight, this can be a handsome room.

I have a good spatial sense, but I am best at color. The way I work, I cover this big square table with color chips and swatches that I keep moving around on the architectural plans. I live for months with all the pieces of the job on this miniature scale before I go ahead. You can learn the principles of creating a palette and mixing and grading color, but the creativity comes from within.

It's the same in the theater. You need to learn the basic skills and technique, but nobody can really *teach* you how to write a melody.

IT GAVE ME great joy to indulge my talent for design by renovating my new home. But I didn't buy the house and do it over as an amusing artistic experiment. This was my *home*. I wanted to create a bright, cheerful place where I would be happy living, working, and entertaining my friends.

And that's what I did. From the day I opened my door and said, "Okay, everybody—my house is ready," there were parties in that house night after night after night.

People were constantly making music in that living room. Carol Dorian spent more time singing at my piano than she did in her own home. My agent at the time, Jack Hutto, who lived about a half block away, was always in that house. I had guests in the guest room all the time. My friend Sheila Mack came to visit one day and she stayed for eleven years as my secretary.

I never became a party-giver the way my parents were natural-born party-givers. But I had Christmas parties and New Year's Eve parties and Halloween parties and all kinds of birthday parties. There were occasional nutty evenings when we would do something silly. I remember one big, hilarious costume party. Sheila and I came as nuns.

People still remember that house as a very smart, glamorous Manhattan townhouse. I remember it more for the lovely warm atmosphere, a house that was filled with work and fun and people. That was the house where I came home, exhausted and happy, from magazine interviews and awards dinners, and all the rest of the *Dolly!* madness.

You have to understand that *Hello, Dolly!* was the biggest thing since sliced bread.

Dolly! was on the cover of *Life* magazine. *Dolly!* was on the cover of *every* magazine. You couldn't turn on a radio without hearing Sammy Davis, Jr., singing "It Only Takes a Moment." You couldn't go to a supper club without the orchestra playing five songs from the show. *Dolly!* even inspired an 1890s fashion trend.

The whole country was caught up in the *Dolly!* fever. There was no way to act blasé about this hysteria. You just had to laugh and enjoy it. Which is exactly what I was doing.

Until I got hit with that lawsuit.

SEVEN

"Penny in My Pocket"

I WAS REALLY a very happy guy at this point in my life. Imagine having this big Broadway show—this incredible, unbelievable, phenomenal megahit—to play with!

There is no happier feeling in the world than going to *your* show in *your* theater. And the St. James Theater became *my* theater. I practically lived there.

I would visit at least three nights a week. Sometimes I would spend all day at the theater and not go back to the Village until late at night. I had my comb and my washcloth and my little bottle of mouthwash in somebody's dressing room. I had a change of clothes stashed in somebody else's dressing room. It felt like home.

Most of the time I would spend backstage. I used to love to sit and gossip with Eileen Brennan and Sondra Lee. I would hang out in Charles Nelson Reilly's dressing room and we'd make each other laugh so hard I was always afraid he would miss his entrance. David Burns was another one who could always make me hysterical with laughter.

But Carol Channing was my best pal. Whenever I went into her dressing room, we would always hug first. Then she would sit me down and fill me in on *everything* that was going on at the St. James. Carol was just like Dolly Levi—she was the center of our world.

Outside our little theater, the whole country was going crazy over *Hello, Dolly!*

Everyone in town and every tourist who came into the city wanted to see the show. They were *storming* the theater for tickets. The St. James holds only 1,600 people, so we were sold out for seven years. It was like a fever sweeping the country. It was wild.

You don't think of these things at the time, but the mass hysteria over this show probably had something to do with the national mood. *Dolly!* was the first big hit after President Kennedy's assassination, and I think that people were desperate to feel happy and hopeful again. They were dying for the cheerful, upbeat sound of a showtune.

Even David Merrick was going around—I can't say he was grinning, because Mr. Merrick would never crack a grin in public—but purring, like a very large black cat licking its whiskers. He was preening like that when he came over to our table at some awards ceremony. He leaned over like he had this big secret, and he said, "The album just made the charts."

The album eventually made it to number one. That flamed the *Dolly!* fever because the Louis Armstrong single was already on every jukebox and radio station in the country. I had the most popular song in the country. You could not turn on the radio to get the weather report without hearing that banjo.

But what was really remarkable—phenomenal, even—was that Louis Armstrong's jazz arrangement displaced the Beatles, who had been number one on the charts for sixteen weeks with "I Want to Hold Your Hand." On the seventeenth week, "Hello, Dolly!" pushed it off. That added tremendously to the cachet of the show.

More important, it showed the world that the Broadway showtune was not dead. In 1964, everybody was so sure that it was the end of the line for show music, that rock music had completely taken over the popular music industry. I can't tell you how tickled I was when we made number one.

IT WAS AN incredibly giddy time and I think we were all punchy. Carol and Charles Lowe and I got through it all by clinging to each other and laughing.

And then the awards started coming in.

The first one was the New York Drama Critics Circle Award, which was very small but very prestigious, because it came from all the big, important critics. There was this cozy ceremony upstairs at Sardi's and we all got these very tasteful little plaques. During the ceremony, Carol and Charles and I sat huddled together, clutching our plaques and grinning at each other like Cheshire cats.

When we got up from the table to leave Sardi's, I kind of shrugged my shoulders and said, "What can possibly happen next?" The three of us burst into giggles and that line became our private joke.

A few days later, the three of us were huddled together in exactly the same way at the Tony Awards. *Hello, Dolly!* swept the Tonys. The show won ten awards, which was unprecedented. At just the right moment, I turned to Charles and Carol and said, "What can possibly happen next?"

That went on for the Drama Desk Awards, the Outer Critics Circle Awards, the Grammy Awards, and I honestly forget what else. Every time the awards started piling up at our table, Charles would nudge me and Carol would giggle, and I would shrug and say, "What can possibly happen next?"

Unhappily, I soon found out.

* * *

ONE DAY, I got a call from my lawyer.

"We have a problem," he said. "A songwriter has filed a complaint that the opening notes of 'Hello, Dolly!' are similar to a song he wrote."

"This is not possible," I told him. I was absolutely bewildered. Since then, I have learned from people in the business that these nuisance suits are a very common occurrence with big hit shows. But at the time, this was news to me. I was flabbergasted.

"Of course it's possible," my lawyer said. "Think about it. There are only eight notes that everybody who writes music *has* to use. How many combinations of those eight notes do you think there are? They are not infinite."

I understood what he meant, because the first bars were similar. But after those opening notes the two songs go off in totally different directions. They were so completely unlike each other that no one would dream of comparing them.

The basic forms were different. This other guy's song was what's called an A-B-A-B song, which has a sung verse and chorus and a repeated verse and chorus. My song has a different form entirely, with two chorus sections. You couldn't find a single thing—the chords, the musical structure, the lyric meter—in common.

"I don't want you to worry about this foolishness," my lawyer said. "But you have to answer me very honestly: Do you know this song?"

Well, this was some hillbilly tune, and of course I had never heard it in my life. It was a published song and it had been recorded, but it was hardly being sung in nightclubs in Manhattan.

My life went on, but this cloud kept hanging over my head.

I began to wonder: Is there something *cursed* about this show that won't let me relax and enjoy what I have created? Am I being taught some kind of lesson?

THE CASE NEVER went to court, but I did have to tell my story to this very tough attorney for the other side. He tried to make it sound like I had heard this song somewhere and had somehow retained the notes in my brain.

"The only notes that stay in my brain are from songs that I love and admire," I said. "And I would never, ever fall in love with a song about the joys of being born and raised in Kansas."

To show them how ridiculous this was, I started to *sing* the ludicrous lines of this song—and the young lady who was recording all this burst out laughing.

I was very proud of my deposition, which I wrote entirely by myself. "It is not *work* for me to write a song," I told them. "It is the easiest and the most natural thing in the world for me, so there is no *need* for me to steal somebody else's notes. Besides, I am an honest man. I would not steal two notes from my own mother."

By this time, I was really angry and I didn't care what it was going to cost me in legal fees. I was entirely in the right, and I was determined to clear my name.

It is a very difficult thing to describe the process of writing a song—and it is just about impossible to explain where a melody comes from. I don't believe that anyone can *teach* you how to write a melody. You can study technique for years and years, but that basic talent is either there or it's not.

Melodies come to me all the time—for no reason and sometimes when I least expect them. I can be sitting at the piano, or I can be walking along some totally uninspiring street like

Eighth Avenue. I would love to say: "Oh, yes, I wrote that song when I was standing at the top of the Eiffel Tower, looking down at the rooftops of Paris." But it just isn't that glamorous. A song is more likely to happen in the shower or in line at the grocery store.

When a melody comes to me I don't usually write it out or put it on tape. I just live with it for a while, playing with it in my head. If it doesn't stay with me, I toss it out.

I must have lost a hundred melodies in my time, but they don't matter to me. I care only about the ones that stay with me and work their way into my heart. When a melody grabs me that way, I may take the time to tape it or write it out. Sometimes I don't even bother, because if it's a melody that I really care about, I will play it from time to time and retain it through the years.

This is just my own little theory, but if I have to really *work* to remember a melody that I was all excited about, I say it's not worth keeping. I will throw it away, like you throw a fish back into the sea if it isn't good enough to make a meal.

But how do you explain all this to some lawyer who accuses you of being so hard up for a melody that you have to steal somebody else's notes?

IT WAS AWFUL, meanwhile, to see this business splashed all over the newspapers. It was mortifying. But at least I was not alone. I got the most generous calls and letters of support from songwriters I didn't even know.

The call I will always remember came from the great Jule Styne. I had never met the man, but he was an idol of mine.

"Listen," he said, in that scratchy voice. "This is Jule Styne. I've been reading about all this garbage that's going on with you, and there's something you ought to know. You have not paid your dues until you go through something like this. We've all been through it. It's an occupational hazard."

Other writers called to tell me their war stories, but Jule Styne had a way of putting it.

"You would have to be out of your mind to steal somebody else's work," he said. "But we're all working with the same eight notes. Somebody's *bound* to repeat something, especially if you write in a simple, direct style—which is the best way to write, anyway. The only way you can be safe is if you write strange, quirky stuff."

Jule Styne was the one who put it in perspective for me. He told me that Irving Berlin had a problem like this. The Gershwins were bothered, too. He showed me how "Oh, You Beautiful Doll" is "I'm Just Breezing Along with the Breeze"—note for note. One of Jule's own songs, he told me, this gorgeous thing called "Ride on a Rainbow," he later discovered was the exact verse of "All the Things You Are."

I can give you another example of how easy it is to unknowingly use a series of notes that have been used before. The first eight notes of "The Way He Makes Me Feel," which is a song from the score of the Streisand movie *Yentl*, are identical note by note to the first eight notes of my song "Ribbons Down My Back," which had been written years earlier. I never even mentioned this fact—no less instituted a lawsuit—because Michel Legrand, who wrote the *Yentl* score, is an entirely ethical writer whom I admire enormously. It was obviously purely unconscious on his part.

Jule Styne finished up his pep talk by saying, "Anyway, kid, I just want you to know that there is not a soul in this business who doesn't want this lousy thing settled in a week, so you can get back to your business."

It could have worked out that way. It *should* have worked out that way. But Hollywood had caught the *Dolly!* fever, and that changed everything.

*   *   *

ALL THE MAJOR film companies were begging for the film rights to *Hello, Dolly!,* but we were in serious negotiations with Twentieth Century–Fox. They were prepared to do a lavish, expensive film of the show, and they were offering us the best deal.

The negotiations were going beautifully—until the studio heard about this lawsuit business. The legal department of Twentieth Century–Fox was very polite, but very firm: "We can't complete these documents," they told us, "while there is a legal cloud over the property."

That's when my phone *really* started ringing. I think Gower Champion was the first one.

"Jerry," he said, "my heart is broken for you. This must be even more painful for you than everything you went through in Detroit. But we've all worked very hard, and you've got to see that this is our big chance to make some real money."

"Gower," I said, "I would never stand in the way of my friends and collaborators. Let me think about this."

Then Michael Stewart, who was like my brother, came to me.

"I don't know how to say this," he told me, "but this may be our only chance. Styles change so fast in Hollywood. One minute musicals are popular, the next minute they're not. If we don't make this movie deal now, we may never get another chance. Can't you just settle this business?"

I told him, "I want to resolve this more than anybody. But if I settle out of court I can't fight these charges. I can't even *try* to speak up for myself."

Marge Champion talked to me. Everybody talked to me. Even Thornton Wilder's people came to me and said, "How can you take away this man's income?"

Don't get me wrong—nobody was badgering me. They

were all very kind. They just made me feel that I had to straighten this out, and do it fast, or we would all lose about $3 million dollars. And I would be responsible.

I can't say that it was my decision to settle, because I really had no other choice. I could not alienate all the people I had worked with. I could not stop their income—or my own, either, because I wanted this movie deal to go through as much as anyone else.

So we settled out of court for $200,000. Today, that sum does not sound enormous, but in those days that was a fortune for me. I paid the $200,000 and it was over.

Do I regret not having fought the suit? The answer is: yes. I would *love* to have taken a stand and defended myself. It still bothers me that I didn't get that chance. So in a way, that painful chapter in my life was never closed.

ONE WEEK AFTER we settled the case, the contract with Twentieth Century–Fox was signed. The cloud was finally lifted. But the gossip and the publicity remained, and that's what really hurt me.

I began to see the unattractive underbelly of the business. There were personal remarks that went around Broadway and a lot of buzzing in the newspaper gossip columns. Today, after a lifetime of creating a body of work, I might just brush off those jabs. But at the time, I was very young and fair game.

There was also some jealousy involved. After all, I was the new boy in town and I had just won a Tony Award in competition with major, major older figures in the Broadway establishment. Almost everybody in the business wished me well, but some people had to resent my success.

A tougher person would have said: "Screw you, everybody!" and shrugged it off. But it was very hard on me, because I was still this kid who just wanted to be loved. I had written this wonderful show and I wanted people to love me for it.

I never really outgrew that need to be liked. Even today, if I know that somebody out there doesn't like me, I want to know why. And I will turn heaven and earth around to get them to like me. That's stupid, because I can't make the whole world think I'm a lovely man. I know I can't do that—but I would like to.

So maybe that's another reason why my music is so cheerful and upbeat. If I can make the whole world happy with my music, maybe the whole world will love me.

Mame WAS MY next project, and I tore into it like a tiger because I had been put through the wringer and hung out to dry with *Dolly! Mame* was my way of saying to the world: "I can do it again. Just watch me!"

Producers were starting to call me, but none of the projects they were offering really thrilled me. Then one day the phone rang and this unfamiliar voice said: "Hello, my name is Jerry Lawrence." Well, I had seen *Inherit the Wind* and *Auntie Mame,* so of course I knew that Jerome Lawrence and Robert E. Lee were brilliant playwrights. But I had no idea what this phone call was about.

"Bob Lee and I would love to take you to lunch," he said. A few days later, we met for lunch at Sardi's. They were very charming gentlemen, and after we made the usual small talk about what was playing on Broadway and the future of the American musical theater, Jerry Lawrence turned to me and said, "How would you like to make a musical out of *Auntie Mame?*"

I didn't have to think about it for a minute. I just yelled out, *"Wow!"*

It was a quiet afternoon in Sardi's and I must have yelled pretty loud, because everybody in the whole restaurant looked around to see what was going on at our table. I felt a little embarrassed at the time, but that *"Wow!"* was a perfect reaction. It was my honest feeling.

When I recovered, I said to Lawrence and Lee: "Yes! My answer is yes. I don't even have to call my agent. I'm just going to *tell* him that I'm doing this show." We shook hands on it.

What an idea that was! *Auntie Mame* was this enormously charming book by Patrick Dennis, the true story about how he was orphaned when he was just a little boy, and how he goes to live with this glamorous, irrepressible aunt who teaches him how to live like a bohemian. People were crazy about this story of Dennis's life, which Lawrence and Lee had turned into a stage play, because the characters were so appealing and because little Patrick's life with his madcap aunt was such an exciting and delicious adventure.

Mame was the show that healed all the wounds from *Hello, Dolly!*

If somebody said to me: "Jerry Herman, you have *got* to come up with some bad story about *Mame,* some big fight or ugly moment," I just couldn't do it. *Mame* was one of the great joys of my life. It was the most warm and wonderful experience, and so completely free of stress that when we were out of town we used to unwind by going to the movies.

I remember sitting in a movie theater in Philadelphia watching Melina Mercouri in *Topkapi.* Angela Lansbury was on one side of me and Beatrice Arthur was on the other side. We were eating popcorn and candy and relaxing just like normal people do at the movies.

In the middle of the film it dawned on me that there was something unnatural about this. I nudged Angela and Bea and whispered: "You know, we're supposed to be going through hell. If anybody we knew saw us right now, they wouldn't believe their eyes."

That's the kind of experience *Mame* was.

EIGHT

"Open a New Window"

MAME DENNIS WAS the best character for a Broadway musical who ever came down the pike. I couldn't *wait* to start writing songs for her. I was so mad for that lady, I could have written three dozen songs for her.

Young composers sometimes make the mistake of thinking they are supposed to write for the star. I certainly believe in making the star comfortable with a song. If the star is at ease with the material, you look good, the star looks good, the show looks good. But you don't ever write for the star, you write for the character.

From my earlier experience with Carol Channing I had learned two lessons: the value of making your star comfortable with a song you've written and the danger of writing that song, or any song, with a certain performer in your mind. No matter how brilliant the star is, writing for a specific performer constricts the writing.

The only honest way to write is to write for the character—and there never was a character as well-suited to the musical stage as Mame Dennis Burnside.

The first thing I had to do was give her an identifying lyric sound, because once I knew what my lady sounded like, that would also become the identifying sound of the piece. So I wrote "It's Today," which establishes her as a madcap, fun-loving lady who has her own set of values—from when to throw a party to when to fight prejudice.

Then I turned to an early scene when young Patrick goes into his Auntie Mame's bedroom the morning after one of those big parties and wakes her up. Mame gets up in a fog, because it's awfully early and she's terribly hung over. But when she finally focuses on this kid she realizes that she has to take charge of his life. So she says to him, "Get dressed, Patrick. We are going out. I am going to show you things you never dreamed existed."

Well, that was *it* for me. Here's what I wrote:

> "Open a new window
> Open a new door
> Travel a new highway
> That's never been tried before
> Before you find you're a dull fellow
> Punching the same clock
> Walking the same tightrope
> As everyone on the block. . . ."

When I finished that song, I knew that I had really found Mame Dennis's voice.

Mame is the type of woman who gets carried away when she gets an idea, and in this song she is literally carried away by her vision of the life that she and Patrick are going to have together. She takes him up this immense spiral staircase and when they get to the very top, the walls of the bedroom fly away and all the most wonderful, exciting things you've ever dreamed about start floating by.

We let our imaginations go wild, inventing all sorts of marvelous adventures for that number. Mame takes Patrick to a fire so he can ride on the fire engine. The two of them dance the tango at a speakeasy, and when the speakeasy is raided, Mame gets to drive the paddy wagon. It was glorious fun.

Once I had written "Open a New Window," the rest of the songs just started pouring out of me. I never wrote more quickly, or with more assurance in my life, because I loved what I was writing. I absolutely loved *Mame*.

I WANTED TO show the affection between Patrick and Mame, so the next song I wrote was "My Best Girl," which Patrick sings after Mame has made a spectacle of herself on stage in a catastrophic operetta.

It's a very sweet and gentle song that also tells you something about young Patrick's character. Mame is all alone on the stage and he knows that she's feeling miserable because the operetta was a debacle and everybody laughed at her. So he walks right up to her and says, "I thought you were wonderful, Auntie Mame." That just broke my heart because it was the simplest, sweetest declaration of love.

After that, I had the great fun of writing "The Man in the Moon" for Bea Arthur to sing in the antique operetta in which she plays a lady astronomer. At the first preview, Bea came right down to the edge of the stage and sang very earnestly and sincerely, directly to the audience:

> "I have a little secret I'd like to impart
> That I hope doesn't give you too much of a start
> Tho' it's shocking, it's completely true
> I know it isn't gossip, or rumor, of course
> For I've had it from quite a reliable source
> And I'd like to pass it on to you."

When she got this far, Bea peered into her telescope, took a loooong pause, looked straight into the front row of the orchestra, and sang:

"The man in the moon is a lady. . . ."

Well, the roar that went up from the audience lasted a full minute. Bea had to stand there forever with that telescope pressed to her eye before the audience would let her go on. Talk about stopping a show . . .

BY THE TIME I wrote that song, I was just *roaring* along with the score. The songs were popping out of me so fast it was like a blur.

People always want to know where songs come from. My answer is always the same: I am inspired by the material. I *need* an *Auntie Mame* or a *La Cage aux Folles* to write that kind of stuff. Nothing less will do it for me, which is why I always say that my toughest job is finding the right source material.

That's why I turn down so many things. I was never a person who wanted to grab everything that people offered to me. I only ever wanted to do what I knew was right for me.

David Merrick offered me a musical version of *The Apartment*, the Billy Wilder movie that starred Jack Lemmon and Shirley MacLaine. I turned it down because it was too contemporary for me.

Contemporary is something I am not. Even today, if you asked me to sit down and write a rap song, or a hip-hop song, I could probably do it, because I can do a pastiche of just about anything. But it would just be a superficial treatment. That kind of material wouldn't be the real me, and that song wouldn't be the real thing.

The Apartment became *Promises, Promises* and it was the real thing, because it was written by Burt Bacharach and Hal David. So even when some of these projects go on to become hits, I don't ever feel that I have lost anything.

There were one or two things, though, that *did* get away from me, and I still have my regrets because the material was so perfect for me. After *Dolly!,* the same team was supposed to get together for David Merrick to do a musical of Billy Wilder's classic film comedy, *Some Like It Hot.* Jule Styne and Bob Merrill turned that into *Sugar,* and it's always been a show I wished I had written.

The other show that I would have truly *loved* to write is *The Rainmaker*. I adore *The Rainmaker,* and I didn't actually lose the show, because it was never offered to me. Harvey Schmidt and Tom Jones did a good job on that material when it became *110 in the Shade.*

In a case like that, you just shrug your shoulders and say: "That was not meant to be." And you walk away.

SOMETIMES THE SONG comes directly from a character's need. "We Need a Little Christmas," which flew off the page, was written because Mame had to turn a disastrous situation into a joyous one.

In that scene, the Depression has hit Beekman Place. The house is bare. There's no furniture and all the paintings and sculpture and fabulous pieces of art work are gone. Mame is wearing a dowdy shopgirl dress and standing in her empty house, when she suddenly pulls out three little presents for Gooch and Ito and Patrick.

They say to her, "What are you doing? It's only November." And she says, "Well, we need it *now!*"

> "Haul out the holly
> Put up the tree

> Before my spirit falls again
> Fill up the stocking
> I may be rushing things
> But deck the halls again now
> For we need a little Christmas
> Right this very minute
> Candles in the window
> Carols at the spinet
> Yes, we need a little Christmas
> Right this very minute
> It hasn't snowed a single flurry
> But Santa, dear, we're in a hurry. . . ."

That was Mame all over. She was telling them that you don't have to go by the rules. Mame Dennis never went by the rules. She made up her own rules. You don't have to wait for a special day to celebrate Christmas. It was more important to celebrate Christmas when you *need* it.

That song brought out inner strengths in that woman that she didn't even know she had—that *I* didn't even know she had.

OTHER SONGS GET written because your collaborators give you the inspiration. That's what happened with "Bosom Buddies."

Lawrence and Lee were from the same school of playwriting as Mike Stewart—congenial and cooperative. They honestly didn't care if I took a line from them and used it for a song, which is how I got my biggest laugh line in "Bosom Buddies." They had written a description of Mame's friend Vera as being "somewhere between forty and death." That was a perfect line for the insult song I was writing for these two old friends, so when Lawrence and Lee graciously let me have their line, I wrote:

MAME: I feel it's my duty to tell you
It's time to adjust to your age
You try to be Peg o' My Heart
When you're Lady Macbeth.
Exactly how old are you, Vera, the truth

VERA: Well, how old do you think?

MAME: I'd say somewhere between forty and death.

The only song I *dreaded* writing was the title song. I felt there was no way I could possibly repeat the success of "Hello, Dolly," which had been a pure phenomenon. So I made the decision that I was not even going to *try* to write a showstopping title song. Instead, I gave myself an incredibly difficult assignment.

I may have made it sound, as one critic wrote, that I shake songs out of my sleeve. Not true. If anybody wants to know how hard I work, they should take a good look at "Gooch's Song."

That's the comedy number that Mame's mousy little secretary sings after she goes out into the world to live—and comes back pregnant. That was probably the most difficult lyric I ever wrote because it is all internal rhyme schemes.

When you work in this scheme, the rhymes don't just come at the ends of the lines, they also come in the middle. I adore the internal rhyme. It is absolutely the classiest kind of lyric you can write because it's a puzzle within a puzzle. That makes my work twenty times more difficult, but also twenty times more satisfying.

I do a lot of walking when I'm writing lyrics. It's an energy thing with me. I think best when I'm moving, and when I'm stuck on a lyric I always get out of the house and go take a walk. My friends are always kidding me that I'm going to get run over because I'm concentrating so hard on rhyming in my head that I might walk into traffic.

Well, I walked up and down New York for *days* writing "Gooch's Song." And every time I hit on something really good, I would stop and buy myself an ice cream cone. That song earned me a gallon of ice cream:

> "Who'd think this Miss Prim would
> Have opened a window
> As far as her whim would allow
> And who would suppose it
> Was so hard to close it
> Oh, what do I do now?
> I polished and powdered and puffed myself
> If life is a banquet, I stuffed myself."

That was *not* one of those songs that just poured out of me. It was an absolute killer of a piece. But the challenge and the sheer fun of it was worth the agony.

It gave me such a thrill when Jane Connell sang "Gooch's Song" so brilliantly. She understood the secret of that song, which is: you cannot sing it as a broad joke, even if you look absolutely ridiculous with your belly out to here. If you treat this as a sad, serious lament, and sing it with sweetness and honesty, you will get twice as many laughs.

> "And so I wandered on
> Till I found my prince
> And have I been nauseous ever since.
> Oh, what do I do now?"

By this time, I was getting very near the end of the writing. And then it suddenly hit me that there was a much deeper emotional layer in this material that had yet to come out.

We had captured all that wonderful madcap fun that was in

the original play and the movie. But I saw that underneath the comedy was a heartrending story of a woman who is betrayed by the child she has brought up. This generous, tolerant woman has taken her little nephew and molded him according to her own avant-garde values. And then one day she turns around and realizes that her little love has grown up and turned into her worst nightmare: a narrow bigot, the very thing she has hated and fought against all her life.

In this context of this show, that moment of recognition is devastating. No one had ever explored that side of Mame—and now I had the chance. If I could write a song that would express Mame's unbearable sense of loss and personal failure, I would not just be adding cute songs to an already cute story. I would be bringing out a whole new aspect of a character everybody thought they knew.

Once I realized my opportunity, I was passionate to write this song.

I started with the image that Mame had of little Patrick when they met for the first time and instantly fell in love. That boy was the most important person in her life, and you have to feel her disappointment and sadness when he grows up and rejects everything she has taught him. Then I let her start thinking of what she might have done wrong herself to corrupt that loving little boy.

The music had to signify that, for the first time in her life, Mame Dennis Burnside is not in charge. Her emotions are taking over and pulling her off center. You get that mood in the bluesy sound of the music. The lowered tones of those diminished chords make the lyrics feel a little sad, a little heart-stopping.

> "Did he need a stronger hand?
> Did he need a lighter touch?
> Was I soft or was I tough?

Did I give enough?
Did I give too much?
At the moment that he needed me
Did I ever turn away?
Would I be there when he called
If he walked into my life today?
Were his days a little dull?
Were his nights a little wild?
Did I overstate my plan?
Did I stress the man
And forget the child?
And there must have been a million things
That my heart forgot to say
Would I think of one or two
If he walked into my life today?
Should I blame the times I pampered him
Or blame the times I bossed him
What a shame I never really found the boy
Before I lost him
Were the years a little fast?
Was his world a little free?
Was there too much of a crowd
All too lush and loud
And not enough of me?
Though I'll ask myself my whole life long
What went wrong along the way
Would I make the same mistakes
If he walked into my life today?"

I don't like separating my music and lyrics, I really don't. But I love every word of that lyric.

I wrote the words and the music to "If He Walked Into My Life" at the same time, and in about a day. I had done exactly what I wanted to do with that material, which was to deepen and enrich it. It was a glorious creative moment for me.

People don't know this, but I have actually won more

awards as a lyricist than I have as a composer. And yet I always feel that people take my lyrics for granted. Maybe it's just harder to get acknowledged as a lyricist, the way that Comden and Green are acknowledged as lyricists, when you write both music and lyrics. Maybe it's because my melodies have become so familiar. I am often introduced as composer Jerry Herman, instead of composer-lyricist Jerry Herman.

Mame did not win the Tony Award in 1966, *Man of La Mancha* did. But *Variety* took a critics' poll that year, and although *Man of La Mancha* still won for Best Music, *Mame* won for Best Lyrics. The *Mame* people were outraged that I lost the Tony, but I was absolutely thrilled that somebody recognized my work as a lyricist. That award truly made me proud.

THE SHOW WAS pretty much finished, and I was still doing everything I could possibly do to avoid writing a title song.

One day, I got this call from Bobby Fryer, who was one of my producers. "Jerry," he said, "can I come over and talk to you?" I said, "Of course," and I asked him when he wanted to come by. "Right now," he said.

When he got to my place in the Village, Bobby came right to the point. The three producers wanted me to write a title song.

"Bobby," I said, "I can't repeat 'Hello, Dolly!' It's never going to happen again, and any half-hearted attempt is going to sound like I'm pushing it. I just don't think I can do it again."

David Merrick would have come after me with a shotgun. Bobby was very sweet about it. He didn't say I *had* to write this song, he said that the producers would be thrilled if I would just *try* to write this song.

"Let me think about it," I said. "If I can come up with something that is fresh and different, I'll try it."

Bobby gave me a big bear hug and left me alone.

It was about three o'clock in the afternoon. I just sat there for a while, thinking how close we were to the show we wanted. We were almost ready to go into rehearsal, and the producers had so much faith in the project they had already booked a theater.

The only thing we didn't have was a star.

And a title song.

THE SCENE THAT came into my mind was the fox hunt down South that turns into a shambles when Mame captures the fox and lets it go. That fox hunt is not for real, it's a spoof. I said to myself, why not do a totally outrageous spoof of the old South? These banjos started playing in my head, and that's what got my juices flowing.

When I do my lyric writing I use these huge pads of thick white paper that I like to scribble all over. When I heard those banjos, I grabbed a pad and the first thing I wrote down was: "You make the bougainvillea turn purple at the mention of your name."

It wasn't even a whole line, but it was all I needed, because once I get the basic idea, I'm off. All these wonderful images kept coming to me. "You coax the blues right out of the horn"—that's so Southern and so sexy. "You charm the husk right off of the corn"—that's so Southern and so corny. I was getting excited.

"Your special fascination'll
Prove to be inspirational
We think you're just sensational,
Mame."

The words and the melody came flying out together and I had the whole song written in about twenty-five minutes. It was 4:15 when I called Bobby Fryer, about an hour after he had left my house. I told him I had a little something that I would polish up and bring over in the morning.

Well, I never changed a hair of that song. I must have played it a hundred times that night and driven my poor neighbors crazy. But every single word and all three choruses stayed exactly the way I wrote them, and that's what I sang for everybody in the producers' Park Avenue office the next morning.

Our director Gene Saks was there, along with our three producers, and Onna White, the choreographer. I played the whole thing, and in my life I never got such a wild reaction. These people started screaming and stamping their feet on the floor. Onna White told me she could see the whole thing staged in her head. Larry Carr, a very tall and elegant man who was one of our producers, threw his arms around me and said, "Jerry, nothing can stop this show now."

So now we had everything—except a star.

I CAN'T LIE about it. Casting the lead for *Mame* was a hair-raising experience.

The producers were so high on the show right from the beginning that they went to the Shuberts and booked the Winter Garden Theater months in advance. We were all so busy finishing the songs and polishing up the script that nobody noticed the deadline was getting perilously close—until it was only about two months away. Suddenly I was told that auditions had to start *immediately*.

What the producers really wanted was a big Broadway name. Somebody like Mary Martin. To tell the truth, we *all* wanted Mary Martin. Bobby Fryer and I had actually gone all the way to Brazil to woo her, but she just didn't want to work.

So there we were.

Well, we started frantically calling in every woman who was alive and breathing and able to act and sing a little bit. It was an endless parade of very interesting and very different women.

Personally, I loved Nanette Fabray's energy and Lisa Kirk's glamour and Dolores Grey's voice and Alice Ghostley's humor—but nobody really hit us in the heart. There was something appealing about each and every one of them, but nobody had Mame's innate elegance. This is a woman who can be sliding down a bannister or playing a bugle and still be an elegant lady.

Gene Saks, our director, told us that we *had* to make a decision soon. We had finally made up our minds to go with either Dolores Grey or Nanette Fabray—I don't think either of those ladies ever knew how close they were—but something held us back.

After one of those call-back auditions I went home and got out my Playbills from all those shows my father and mother had taken me to. I just wanted to see if there was anybody we had missed.

I came across the Playbill for *Anyone Can Whistle,* this lovely Stephen Sondheim show that only ran one week. Suddenly I had this vivid memory of Angela Lansbury singing this terrific song about a parade. I remember that she just *belted* it out. But because of her English background, she also had this very refined quality—a quality of elegance. I suddenly got this good feeling in my heart.

The producers were not terribly interested when I told them they had to fly Angela Lansbury in from Malibu to audition. None of them had seen the Sondheim show, and Larry Carr thought she was too old. "That's the lady that plays everybody's mother in Hollywood," he said.

Angela had just played Laurence Harvey's mother in *The*

Manchurian Candidate. That's what Larry Carr was talking about. But what he didn't know was that Angela was only three years older than Laurence Harvey.

I kept saying how stunning she was, and how young she was, and how we could give her a great haircut and the whole glamour treatment. They weren't convinced. I was getting a little desperate, so I finally asked them to give her an audition just to *humor* me. They did it—but they didn't like it.

THREE DAYS LATER, Angela Lansbury knocked on my door. She had just gotten off the plane from California, and she had come directly to my house because she wanted to get to work. It was a couple of years since she had done any singing—not since *Anyone Can Whistle,* actually.

Angela was nervous about that, but I wasn't. This was a lovely actress who brought with her all that inner elegance she was born with. I knew in ten minutes that she was perfect for Mame.

We worked at the piano all afternoon. She was very quick and a delight to work with, but I didn't want to leave anything up to chance.

"You and I have got to be in cahoots on this audition," I told her. "You are exactly what I have in my head for this role. But we have got to show the others a side of you that they don't know."

"I'll do anything," she said. "I want this part."

So I told her my plan.

"All the other ladies have sung their own material for their auditions," I said. "But if *you* get up there and sing two songs from this score, the producers and the director will fall over. They have only heard my scratchy voice singing these songs. If you can learn two songs by tomorrow you will knock their socks off."

I thought she would be terrified. Any performer would be terrified at the idea of learning two songs in one afternoon. Angela wasn't. She was thrilled—and she loved the idea of being in collusion with the composer.

So we worked and we worked and then we worked some more. I even suggested a little bit of stage business to do with a full-length mink coat. When we finally called a dinner break, Angie, my secretary Sheila Mack, and I all went out to the old Longchamps that used to be on Fifth Avenue, right around the corner from my place.

I remember this first dinner so vividly. We had fabulous seafood dinners and we talked and laughed like old friends. There was something special about this woman, with her cultured voice and exquisite bearing and her wonderful sense of humor. I just fell in love with her.

At some point over dinner, I told Angela the other part of my plan, which was going to be our big secret. During the audition, I would be sitting in my usual seat at the theater. But when the moment came for her entrance, I would excuse myself to go to the men's room. I would then slip into the orchestra pit, where nobody could see me, and I would play the piano for her.

And that's exactly how it went the next morning. There were a lot of people around, because we were seeing other ladies at this audition. But when Angela's moment came, I excused myself, walked up the aisle, and disappeared. Two minutes later, when the stage manager announced "Angela Lansbury," I was already in the pit, sitting at the piano.

Angela walked out on the stage smiling that wonderful smile of hers. Then she tossed her mink on a chair, and gave them all a look. I played her the chord for "It's Today" and she started *belting* out "Light the candles / Get the ice out / Roll the rug up / It's today."

From my position in the pit I couldn't see their faces. But I just knew that their jaws were dropping. Then, before anybody could say anything, I swung into the second song we had rehearsed, "If He Walked Into My Life." I never took my eyes off Angela, and I could see that she was really *acting* this song. I couldn't see the rest of them, but I figured they were all on the floor by now.

At the end of the song, I popped up from the pit and gave them all a big grin. By this time, everybody knew that it had been a huge setup. But they were so impressed with Angela that it really didn't matter.

And of course, she got the part.

NINE

"My Best Girl"

WORKING ON *MAME* was like having a love affair. Not only was I passionately in love with the show, but I was drawn into the rehearsals and made to feel part of everything that went on with the production.

You get some real dictators in this business, especially with directors and choreographers. But Gene Saks, our director, and Onna White, our choreographer, were much happier guiding us than dictating to us. Gene was a strong director, but he wasn't an overbearing director who had to hold the reins. His collaborative style of working made him less of a boss and more of a team member.

Onna also went out of her way to make me feel that she really cared what I thought. At rehearsals she used to save a seat for me right next to her. Whenever I poked my head in her dance studio, she would point to the empty chair and wave me in, so she could show me what she was doing. And she always listened to what I had to say.

You have to remember that I had just come off a show with Gower Champion, who worked in a very insular way. Gower didn't want anybody around when he was creating something. He would have been happier if you stayed out in the hall.

Gower was a genius, and I respected his privacy because that's the way he needed to work. But I would rather create something from scratch with a director. I think you come out of it with a more satisfying experience and a more unified piece of work.

It was so refreshing to work that way on *Mame*. It made the whole thing such a joy.

With my background in design, it was only natural for me to take a special interest in the show's visual look.

William and Jean Eckart, our set designers, were considered very avant garde for that time. They went for odd, interesting effects—like those abstract images they created for "Open a New Window"—that gave the show the fluid sense we wanted. I felt that the costume designer, Bobby MacIntosh, really cared about my taste and my sensibility. He was always saying to me: "Well, do you like the green velvet on Angela? What do you think about burgundy?" And I was so flattered that Tharon Musser, who is one of Broadway's legendary lighting directors, always asked me to sit in when she was designing a scene.

It was a wonderful rehearsal period. I made a good friend in John Bowab, who was a production assistant on the show. John later became a respected television director of shows like "The Cosby Show" and "It's a Living," but he always had a special affection for *Mame*. He went on to direct countless productions of the show all over the world.

The comfortable atmosphere and our collaborative way of working paid off in Philadelphia, where we took the show for tryouts.

YOU NEVER KNOW what you have with a show until you get out of town. For *Milk and Honey*, I wrote two songs in Boston.

For *Dolly!*, I wrote half the show in Detroit. When *Mame* got to Philadelphia, I had to cut two songs.

Killing something that you have created is one of the hardest things in the world. It's like picking which of your children are going to get on the lifeboat. It was even harder with *Mame,* because the show was such a big hit with the out-of-town audience.

The audience at the first preview was so carried away, they did everything but rip out the seats. Bea was brilliant, they roared every time she opened her mouth, and we could tell that Angela had the potential to become a major star. That first performance was also a triumph for Onna, because she had turned the title song into a fabulous first-act finale. When that curtain came down, the audience *sailed* out for intermission.

Our joy lasted until the traditional morning-after meeting, when Gene Saks told us the show was twenty minutes too long. Twenty minutes is dangerously long, *perilously* long for a Broadway musical.

"Now, look," Gene said. "We have something very special here, so we are not going to chop it up. We are not going to change it. What we need here is some *judicious* cutting that will not harm the fabric of the piece. And we are going to make those cuts one or two minutes at a time."

I loved Gene for that. He didn't panic. He didn't take out a hatchet. He didn't make us feel that we had written bad material. He just asked for suggestions.

"We could get rid of 'Camouflage' and pick up three minutes right there," I said. This was a cute song for Bea and Angela about dressing Mame up as a conventional mother, but we really didn't need it because we already had a strong comedy number in "Bosom Buddies."

That got the ball rolling. Lawrence and Lee brought in lots of little cuts within individual scenes. We never made more than one change each night, so the actors wouldn't have to struggle. I don't care what some directors try to tell you; when you give the actors a lot of changes, you can always see them struggling.

The hardest cut for me was getting rid of the scene and the song that preceded the title song, which was positioned as the first-act finale. In this scene, Mame tells Patrick that she has fallen in love. The little boy wants to know what that means, so Mame sings "Love Is Only Love" to explain that emotion.

"Don't look for shooting stars, because love is only love," the lyric goes. "You touch, but still you touch the ground."

It was a lovely song and nobody did it better than Angela. That was her specialty, those emotionally rich songs that she could really *act*. This was such a charming moment, I just hated to lose it.

Gene handled the whole thing with his usual regard for a person's feelings. He brought it up privately, when we were having hamburgers at this place near the theater that was like our private office. By this time, we had dropped about fifteen minutes from the show by doing these tiny razor cuts. But we still needed one more hunk, and we both knew that we weren't going to get it with razor cuts.

"What do you think would happen," he said, "if we just *tried* the show for one night without that whole scene." I told him very honestly that I would feel terrible about losing that moment. Then I said, "But I trust you. So go ahead and try it." He did. That night, without the scene, the show just *roared* along like a steam engine.

I WAS SORRY to see that song go, but I didn't have to mourn it forever, because songs are living things. If you put them in a nice warm hothouse and don't forget about them, many of them can have a second life.

Writers call that storage place their "trunk." It's where you stash unfinished material and songs that never went anywhere and also your ideas. My trunk is a huge, messy lateral-file cabinet. It is just *stuffed*. I don't go into it very often, but it's a nice feeling when you know you have some things tucked away. It's like having a security blanket.

"Love Is Only Love" came out of storage when Barbra Streisand was making the film version of *Dolly!* The first thing she needed was that patter song, "Just Leave Everything to Me," which I wrote especially for her. She also wanted a ballad for Dolly to sing—and when I went to my trunk, there was "Love Is Only Love."

As much as I liked that song when it was in *Mame,* I had to admit that the first act played better in Philadelphia without that scene. With twenty minutes gone, the show was as tight and sharp as it was ever going to get. We were ready to come into New York.

That called for a celebration, so a group of us went out to dinner: Angie and her husband Peter Shaw, Bea Arthur and Gene Saks, who was her husband at that time, and me. We went to this wonderful old Philadelphia restaurant called Bookbinder's that was famous for its seafood.

We all sat down and the first thing Bea did was to order a drink. "I am terribly sorry," the waiter told her, "but we have a state law here that we cannot serve alcohol on a Sunday." Poor Bea groaned.

After the waiter left with our order, Peter Shaw said, "I hear that some restaurants in this town will serve you a drink in a teacup." So the next time the waiter came to our table, Bea looked up at him and bellowed, "Tell Mr. Bookbinder to bring me a cup of vodka!"

SOME OF THE songs from the show were already out on the air when we arrived at the Winter Garden in the spring of 1966 for previews. It was still those days when many singers depended on Broadway scores for their material and when music publishers put out demo records of new show scores. Our publisher had gone nuts and put out a gorgeous demo of *Mame,* very lavish with lots of instruments. There was very good pickup.

I don't remember all the performers who made records, but they were blaring out of every record store on Broadway when we got into town for our week of previews.

The biggest hit was Bobby Darin's jazzy single of "Mame." That recording was getting a lot of play on radio stations and it was coming up on the charts before the show even opened. An instrumental version by Mantovani was also very popular. Somebody else gave the show a boost by singing "Mame" on "The Ed Sullivan Show," which was a very good place to showcase material in those days.

The point is that people already knew the title song before the show opened. That builds up the interest in a new musical and adds to the excitement of a big Broadway opening—or it used to, anyway.

I WAS STANDING in the back of the theater for the opening night of *Mame* at the Winter Garden when Don Pippin came out. Don was our new musical director and an absolute genius with a showtune. He would remain my musical director for all my other shows and become my right hand in this business. I found in Don a man who completely understood my style, my perfect musical soulmate.

On his way to the orchestra pit, Don noticed his father sitting in the third row. He smiled and gave his father a little nod of recognition. The elder Mr. Pippin was so thrilled that he turned to the gray-haired gentleman sitting next to him, who was an absolute stranger to him, and said, "That's my son conducting." The stranger smiled back and said, "He's conducting my son's music."

Don raised his baton to start the overture and that next moment was pure magic. The orchestra got as far as "Mame," and then the entire audience applauded. They recognized the song from all the airplay—and their applause told me that they already knew it and liked it.

I'm not ashamed to say that when I heard that applause, I started bawling. With the new musical styles and the new audience tastes, I don't know if that moment of recognition is still possible on Broadway.

The next morning, I woke up to a wonderful, silly surprise from my pal, Sue Mengers.

When I met Sue, she was a William Morris secretary. She was a very funny lady with great ambition, and I always knew that something extraordinary would happen for her. Sue would later go on to become a very big, very famous Hollywood agent, but in those days she was my theater date. We went to opening nights together throughout the 1960s and she would always make me laugh.

Sue always used to kid around about the two of us getting married. She would say, "Oh, just to be able to walk down this aisle at the next opening, and have everybody point and say: 'There goes Mrs. Jerry Herman.' " It wasn't serious, because she knew I was gay, but we used to giggle about what a fine married couple we would make.

So the morning after *Mame* opened, the doorbell rang and here was this young man from Schrafft's, all dressed up in his cap and uniform to deliver his package. It was an enormous three-tiered wedding cake, very traditional, with all those sugared rosettes and swags. And on the top there was a little bride and groom and the message: "Love, Sue."

*   *   *

MAME OPENED IN 1966, and in those days a showtune could live for a lifetime. That happened with "If He Walked Into My Life."

Eydie Gormé had gotten hold of the publisher's demo, and she fell in love with that song. Don Costa did this incredible arrangement for her practically overnight, and they whisked her right into a studio to record it. That's the way people did things then, as quickly as that.

I was busy with the opening, so I was not part of that recording at all. I never even *heard* the recording until a couple of weeks after the show opened.

A friend of mine called up one day and said, "I have got to come over right away. I have something I want to play you." He came running over to my place in the Village and he put this thing on my record player. And there it was, in all its glory. I was speechless.

To this day, I think that Eydie Gormé's version of "If He Walked Into My Life" is the finest single recording of any song of mine. It is truly exquisite, and it has not aged a hair. That record could have been cut this morning.

Eydie Gormé is a brilliant song stylist and the way she did this song perfectly mirrored what I had in mind—but *perfectly*. She sang everything that I wrote, exactly the way I wrote it, and she did it very straightforwardly. No bending of the notes, or anything like that. Her full-throated delivery is what made it come out like a real torch song. That, and her heartfelt passion for the song. It's the passion that gives you the goosebumps.

Usually, it takes years for a song to become a true standard. But I knew instantly that "If He Walked Into My Life" would be around for years and years, even after I was not.

It's a wonderful thing to watch a song take off like that and become a living thing that can exist on its own. The first thing that happens is that every orchestra in the city picks it up and plays it. I'm talking about huge pops orchestras and little six-piece orchestras and orchestras that play weddings and bar mitzvahs. After that, the song gets recorded in all the anthologies and *everybody* wants to sing it. There were so many male performers who wanted to sing "If *She* Walked Into My Life," I had to write a male version of the lyrics. One day, the music publisher starts sending you recordings of the song in foreign languages. Finally, it becomes everybody's audition song.

While all that was happening, a great actress was giving the most incredible emotional performance of "If He Walked Into My Life" every night at the Winter Garden Theater. The audience always lost it when she sang that song. They saw their own lives and how they felt about their own children, the people they loved. She was heartbreaking.

So NOW I had two theaters to visit every night. I would usually spend the first act at the Winter Garden and watch the "Mame" number. During intermission, I would stroll over to the St. James to catch the "Dolly" number. At the curtain I would go backstage at both shows to make my visits to the various dressing rooms. I would always end up in the chorus dressing room.

These visits were my way of socializing, and they were great fun for me. But they were also a way of keeping an eye on my shows. A long-running show is a very difficult thing to keep in A-one shape. So if I ever heard sloppy singing or noticed liberties of any kind being taken, I would immediately straighten things out.

Mame took off right from the start, and after about a month the hysteria had built to its height. Louis Armstrong picked that moment to come out with his own recording of the title song, and that kept the excitement going. Everybody involved in the show was getting all kinds of attention. Including me.

By this time I wasn't so terrified of the radio and television interviews, the way I had been with *Dolly!,* which is probably because I was getting used to them. I even went on "The Ed Sullivan Show" to sing a medley of my songs with the Mc-Guire Sisters, who were the hottest girl trio around at that time. We were some act, this shy little guy with the nothing voice, singing with this famous trio. But the McGuires helped me get over my fear of performing and they made what could have been a very nerve-wracking evening real fun for me. Years later, when I was performing my own nightclub act at Rainbow and Stars, I thought of my little routine with the McGuire Sisters and I had to smile.

Then we hit the jackpot—we made the cover of *Life* magazine.

When *Mame* was playing on Broadway, *Life* magazine still was *the* magazine. Nobody in America did not read *Life* magazine. And there we were—"Broadway's Best Musical"—on this double cover page that pulled out into a big, beautiful color photograph. It's a gorgeous picture of Angela in her gold lounging pajamas, doing her crazy Groucho imitation and looking so young and radiant. I had that photograph framed and it is still up on my wall.

Mame had everything going for it, including the biggest billboard in the world. For the whole five years of the run, there was no way you could miss this billboard over the Winter Garden, which was not only gigantic, but bright, bright yellow.

I am reminded of the color yellow because that was the color of my face when I got terribly, terribly sick.

One night, I went out to dinner with my agent, Jack Hutto, and my secretary, Sheila Mack. We went to this little restaurant in Chinatown that someone had recommended to me. Jack and I ordered some kind of sweet-and-sour clam dish and Sheila had something else. The clams were delicious and I lapped them up.

Cut to fourteen days later. I was in New Orleans, seeing Mardi Gras with a friend of mine and having a wonderful time—when I suddenly felt very, very ill. It got progressively worse that whole day and night, and I finally had to say to my friend, "I have to go home. I have never felt so bad in my entire life." I was so weak, it felt like all my blood had been drained right out of me.

My friend looked at me and said, "You look very strange, Jerry." He packed my things, got me to the airport, and put me on a plane. When I got to New York, Sheila Mack and Carol Dorian were waiting at the airport with an ambulance. I was so woozy that I could not walk off the plane.

Sheila and Carol knew exactly what this horrible disease was—hepatitis—because Jack Hutto was already in the hospital with it. It was the kind of hepatitis that takes exactly fourteen days to go through your system and Jack had beaten me into the hospital by one day. He was in Lenox Hill, but they took me to Flower Fifth, so I didn't even have the fun of visiting with my poor agent so we could laugh about this disaster. But I was able to call him on the phone every day, because it took about two months in the hospital to get over this thing.

That was the first and only time in my life that I had ever been hospitalized. Hepatitis is a very serious disease that saps all your energy, and I had been running around in New Orleans, eating all kinds of food and exhausting myself. I was a very sick young man.

After they got the worst of this thing out of my system I began to perk up, and the first thing I did was change hospitals. I was so weak they couldn't even put me in a wheelchair. They had to strap me on a gurney and get me into an ambulance.

Sheila Mack had come to the hospital to help me move all my books and presents. But she got very concerned because I looked so awful, and they let her ride with me in the ambulance. Well, I must have looked ghastly. They had me all wrapped up in sheets so I wouldn't get cold. There was even this white sheet wrapped around my head, just like a mummy. All you could see was my face, which was the color of a daffodil.

Sheila must have been petrified. She was holding my hand so tightly it hurt. Her face was dead-white and she was on the verge of tears. We must have driven about a mile in this awful silence, until I turned to Sheila and said to her, very quietly, "Sheila, you have never lied to me, have you?" And she said, "No, of course not, Jerry." And I said, "And you are not going to lie to me now, are you, because I have a very serious question to ask you." And she said, "Absolutely not. Ask me anything you want." And I said, "Tell me the truth—is this a hearse?"

Well, she let out this high-pitched scream of laughter, and I laughed so hard I must have put myself back two weeks. We screamed so loud, they actually stopped the ambulance in the middle of Second Avenue and ran back to open the doors. The two medics stuck their heads in, afraid I might have perished back there. They found the two of us hysterical with laughter.

ONCE I GOT into the new hospital, which was New York Hospital, my body was still weak, but my spirits picked right up. My friends got me the grandest suite in the entire hospital. It was a corner room overlooking the East River, with sofas and nice furniture so you could really enjoy the view. Sheila and Carol put up posters of *Dolly!* and *Mame* and decorated the place with flowers so it would look nice and cheerful.

The hepatitis wasn't contagious, so everybody in the world

came and visited me. I received them like I was holding court, sitting up in this huge bed in this grand suite. The nurses always went gaga when Angela came to visit, and Carol Channing used to keep everybody entertained when she and Charles came by. It was like a party. All we needed was a piano.

All the doctors could do was monitor me as I got a little bit stronger every day, so it was a very long, slow recovery period. But I wouldn't call it painful, because the treatment in those days was a diet of foods very high in fat. Every afternoon at three o'clock the nurse would bring me a huge malted, and being the biggest chocolate maniac of all time, I was in heaven. Plus, my friends all knew that I had to eat this kind of stuff to get well, so they would bring me all kinds of rich, sweet goodies. I stuffed myself until I got a belly.

When I finally got out of the hospital it was the beginning of summer. Sheila insisted that I go out to Fire Island to recuperate at this house I had in the Pines. She came out to cook for me and take care of me, because I still couldn't walk.

So that's how I spent the summer, doing my therapy and slowly recovering. It was actually a wonderful summer, because everybody I knew was out there and people were always dropping by my house to visit.

That was a great beach house. I designed it and had it built in 1962, and I have many memories of good times in that house. I remember one birthday party when Monique Van Vooren showed up in a mini-mini metallic bikini and Carol Channing arrived by helicopter—wearing English golfing knickers.

Sue Mengers was another party girl. She was the exact opposite of Janet Roberts, this proper lady who was a rival talent agent at the William Morris agency. Sue loved to come out to Fire Island and swim in my pool. She was out there once, swimming around naked, when these male friends from next door came over to visit. They were all standing on this upper deck that overlooked the pool and it didn't bother Sue a bit. She just stood up and waved at them: "Hi, there!" she yelled. "My name is Janet Roberts."

I don't know if that funny story ever got back to Miss Roberts, who is a dear lady, but I truly hope it did so she could enjoy the joke too.

Fire Island was heaven, and by my birthday, which is July 10, I was out of the wheelchair and starting to walk. By the end of August I was back up to my normal 135 pounds and feeling just fine.

And that was the end of my ordeal. I'm a little embarrassed to make it sound so glamorous—but it was.

TEN

"Hundreds of Girls"

I WANT TO confess my love—my passion, really—for Judy Garland. This is important to me, because I never got to express my adoration of this great lady in the way that I wanted to—by giving her the role of Mame Dennis.

Judy Garland wanted to replace Angela Lansbury in *Mame*. The show had been running about a year and a half and Angela was talking about doing a little tour and then leaving to do other things. We all expected this day to come, but it was still very sad, because she was the perfect Mame. No one ever gave a better performance.

But when I got word from the William Morris Agency that Judy Garland was interested in replacing Angela, I just about lost my mind.

To understand how I felt when I got this news, you have to know that I was the craziest, the most ardent Judy Garland fan of all time. I still am. I worshipped that woman. It was a passion that went beyond reason. It was purely emotional, because she pressed a button in me that nobody else ever had. She sang, and it was a religious experience for me.

The experience was everything that I love about show business. It was joyous. It was touching. It was bigger than life. When she hit some of those notes, the sound was so thrilling I would hold onto my chair and stop breathing. I would get lost in her voice.

This passion goes back a long way. When I was a kid growing up in Jersey City, a Judy Garland concert could get me out in a blizzard. I mean that literally. One night, when she was giving her one-woman show in Philadelphia, I got into my little jalopy and drove through a terrible snowstorm to get there.

I would do anything, go anywhere for the thrill I got when Judy sang. My best friends Carol Dorian and Phyllis Newman usually went with me on these religious pilgrimages. I was at every performance of her Palace Theater engagement, and of course I was at that famous Carnegie Hall concert. My friends had to hold me by the ankles so I didn't fall out of the balcony.

So now you can understand how I felt when I heard that Judy Garland wanted to play Mame.

THE MINUTE I got the news, I launched a one-man campaign to get her the part.

It wasn't enough that I wanted her, I had to get the excitement going in a lot of other people. I had to convince the producers, Joe and Sylvia Harris, Bobby Fryer, and Larry Carr, plus my collaborators Jerry Lawrence and Bob Lee, along with our director Gene Saks and our choreographer Onna White. All these people had to be with me.

I don't think anyone could have made a better case for her, because it wasn't just the image of Judy Garland that I loved, it was her talent. I think she was a great actress as well as a great singer, and I loved her as a dancer. I was thinking about that recently, when I happened to see a clip of that amazing dance routine she did with Gene Kelly in *Summer Stock*. She was a hell of a dancer.

I honestly think that Garland would have been an absolutely brilliant Mame. I believe that she had the humor, the pathos, the acting style, the dancing ability, and, of course, that incredible voice, to do the part. I can just hear her singing "It's Today" and "If He Walked Into My Life." There would have been pandemonium in the theater—starting with me.

Many, many meetings were held with Miss Garland and all the powers-that-be. She was very charming and she genuinely wanted to do this show. I also think that she was trying very hard to be "good," in a professional sense. She believed in her heart that she would be there every night, faithfully.

Unfortunately, this happened to be one of those periods when Judy was having personal problems, and there were rumors of drinking. Her television show was wonderful but fraught with emotional moments, and I think it is fair to say that Miss Garland had a reputation for not being reliable.

Anyway, the producers and the director came to me and said, "We are very sorry, Jerry, but we cannot do it. We cannot entrust this show to Miss Garland. We have the backers to consider, and we cannot risk a show that is at its peak and has many more years to go. If it all falls apart because she doesn't show up on opening night, we will have destroyed everything that we all worked so hard to create."

I looked right back at them and said, "I don't care! Even a *bad* performance from Judy Garland would be an event. Just to have Judy Garland in this show for *one night* would be magical—historical."

That's how nuts I was. I said all kinds of foolish things, because I wasn't thinking about the practical side of the business. In retrospect, I realize that it was my heart speaking, not my head. The producers did the correct thing. They were protecting their show—and *my* show. So they turned down Judy Garland.

Well, she was destroyed. Liza told me later that her mother was absolutely devastated to be turned down for a replacement role in a Broadway musical. She told Liza her heart was broken, because she knew how *right* she was for it.

That is something that I have had to carry in my own heart through the years. This was a woman I truly idolized. I still can't bear to think of how she was hurt because of something I wrote. It was a very sad experience for me and I have always felt bad about it, because I never wanted to cause that woman pain.

After that, you'd think that Judy would never want to sing anything I wrote, but she actually did do a couple of things of mine. When she did her Palladium concert, she and Liza opened the show with "Hello, Dolly!" I also understand that she once sang "If He Walked Into My Life," in a concert that I never saw, but oh, how I wish I had.

And of course, she continues to be a tremendous influence on my work. She really was the little girl with the big voice who was cruelly overused by MGM. She had that ingenuous quality of the girl next door you wanted to cherish and protect.

But more than anything else, Judy Garland stood for show business, in all its emotional, theatrical glory. I still hear that sound when I write.

THE ONLY GOOD thing that came out of the whole unhappy experience was my lovely relationship with Judy's daughters, Liza and Lorna.

Liza knew that I was really plugging for her mom and she

146

loved me for that. That cemented a warm friendship that has lasted for years.

Liza is one of the nicest people I know. She's a sweetheart. It's not easy being the daughter of a great star. The pressures are cruel, but Liza has a lot of guts and, most important, her own unique talent. I would just fall on the floor if she ever did a show of mine. There is nobody alive who can do my material the way Liza can.

The other thing about Liza, she's such *fun*. You know you're going to have a good time when Liza is around. She is very close to Michael Feinstein, so she came to the studio to visit when we were recording *Michael Feinstein Sings the Jerry Herman Songbook*. The three of us sat down and giggled for hours, like three kids in a college dorm. That's the kind of relationship we have.

Lorna Luft is the kind of friend you can just pick up with, even after years of separation, and feel that same warm closeness. Lorna, Leslie Uggams, and Lee Roy Reams and I once went out on tour in a concert version of my work. We drove from city to city for months on this huge, air-conditioned bus that became our home. Between Leslie's charm, Lorna's dry sense of humor, and Lee Roy's endless show business stories, they made what could have been a grueling experience into a fun-filled adventure.

We usually played very big, classy venues on this tour. But one night, we found ourselves in an auditorium in Punta Gorda, Florida, where they were actually wheeling in the audience. Lorna peeked through the curtain at the house and then came running over to me. "My God, Jerry," she said, "we're in an old-folks' home!" The audience turned out to be very warm and appreciative, but how we ever got through that performance I'll never know. And all I have to do today to get gales of laughter out of Lorna is to say the words: "Punta Gorda."

*   *   *

WHEN YOU THINK about it, my life has been filled with friendships with some of the most talented and interesting women in
the world.

I'm sure this has something to do with my being an only
child and a mama's boy and gay and all that. But that doesn't
make my feelings any less sincere. I like women. I always have.
I like talking with them. I like laughing with them. I truly love
women, and I don't just mean the big stars I have worked
with. Starting with my mother and my Aunt Belle, my closest
friends have always been women.

I met my best friend Carol Dorian on my first day in college,
and we stayed friends for forty years. Carol and I laughed our
way through the rest of her life, like college kids who never
grew up. We never lost that laughter, that craziness that kept
us young. I didn't grow out of that until just a few years ago,
when Carol died over Christmas of a heart attack.

Carol's daughter, Jane Haspel, kind of took her place in my
heart. I am a godparent to both Jane and her five-year-old
daughter Sarah, and they both fill my life with laughter and
love, the way that Carol did for so many years. Jane, her husband David, and Sarah live two blocks away and they are always coming over to my house for tea parties because Sarah
loves tea parties. We let her pour.

It was thanks to Carol Dorian that this sweet, shy gentleman
you know as Jerry Herman was once kicked out of Radio City
Music Hall.

Carol and I had gone to Radio City with a couple of friends
to see a film. This was still the days when they put on a stage
show before they showed the movie, and there were always a
couple of novelty acts before the Rockettes came out to dance.
Now, you have to understand that the novelty acts at Radio

City were truly awful. Dogs jumping through flaming hoops, that sort of ridiculous stuff. We sat through a couple of those acts until this tall, skinny man in a Latin costume came out and proceeded to play the castanets while the symphony orchestra in the pit played Ravel's "Bolero." Then, in the middle of his act, he pulled out a pair of very long shears and he started doing his Bolero act with these silly-looking scissors.

It was so truly ludicrous and the man was so terribly serious, that I just couldn't help myself. I started giggling. And of course, that got Carol started. By now, the orchestra was into it hot and heavy. The music got wilder and wilder, and the man was clicking his scissors in some kind of crazy frenzy. Carol and I were giggling so hard we were both choking.

There is this Jewish word—*mohel*—for the rabbi that performs circumcisions on baby boys. I leaned over to Carol and I whispered, "Look, Carol—a dancing *mohel!*" Well, she screamed so loud that our friends got up and changed their seats, they were so mortified. This was not a giggle or a laugh that I am talking about, but a high-pitched scream that could shatter your eardrums. People started yelling at us, ushers came running down the aisle with flashlights, and pretty soon we found ourselves out on the sidewalk, still shrieking with laughter.

Nobody had a laugh like Carol. We had a lifetime of laughter.

As I BECAME more successful in my career, it was only natural that the direction of my life would change—but not my friendships. They didn't change at all. I made new friends along the way, but I didn't toss out the old ones, because my friends are the most important people in my life. I am a person without mother or father, without brothers or sisters. With the exception of my darling cousin-once-removed Millicent and six first cousins, my family has dwindled to practically nothing. Did you know that Jerry Bock, the superb composer of *Fiddler on the Roof* and *She Loves Me,* is my second cousin!

When I think of family, I think of people like Alice Borden, who was the girl who sang for all my important backers' auditions, including *Dolly!* and *Mame.* Alice and her mother were very close to me and my mother, back when we spent our summers at Stissing Lake, which makes her one of my few remaining friends who loved Ruth Herman and still remembers her. Today, Alice lives in Sherman Oaks, here in California. I see her often, and I am on the phone with her every other day.

One of the dearest members of my family is Sylvia Herscher, who has been so close to me all these years, and so supportive. She was my publisher for a while, and then she was my agent for a while. But more than anything she has been my confidant and my loyal friend.

Sylvia was the one who taught me that a good showtune never dies. When *Hello, Dolly!* had just opened, and everybody in the world was singing the title song, I said to her, "Why isn't anybody recording 'It Only Takes a Moment,' which is my favorite song from that show?" I just couldn't understand why that song, which had a very romantic lyric, didn't get more attention.

> "He held me for an instant
> But his arms felt safe and strong
> It only takes a moment
> To be loved a whole life long.
> And that is all that love's about
> And we'll recall when time runs out
> That it only *took* a moment
> To be loved a whole life long."

Sylvia said to me, "Stop worrying. Songs are living things. All you have to do is put them out there and sooner or later someone will find them." The funny thing is, two weeks later she called me to say, "Jerry, I have in my hand a new Sammy Davis, Jr., album—and on it he does 'It Only Takes a Moment' as a jazz waltz."

My friendships are what it's all about for me. Some of them go all the way back to childhood. I have stayed close with old friends from New Jersey like Elaine and Mort Erenstein, and Claire and Stanley Tannenbaum. And if you want to know how far back some of these friendships go, Claire used to walk me to school when we were little.

For all the women in my life, some of my best pals are men I have known for years. I met my friend Mark Reiner twenty-five years ago, and what a time we've had! Mark owns a successful casting company in Manhattan and has cast many of my productions, including the latest *Hello, Dolly!* But he is also a great traveling companion, and for years we used to go on these wonderful motorcycle runs in upstate New York and Pennsylvania. We would meet up with a whole gang of friends and live outdoors in tents for a whole weekend.

The company was fun, but these campgrounds had the most primitive facilities. So Mark and I would drive up early and surreptitiously check into this little motel a few miles from the campsite. Every day we would manage to sneak away for an hour to shave, shower, brush our teeth, change our clothes, and generally freshen up. By Sunday night, after watching three hundred guys get raunchier and raunchier, Mark and I always looked like we just stepped out of a bandbox. Those guys never learned our secret.

I made many lasting friendships over the summers I spent at Fire Island in the late sixties. One of these good friends is Michael Valenti. When I first met Michael, he told me he was a composer and said that he would like to play some of his work for me. I was so impressed that I introduced him to Gerry Oestreicher, who was my first Broadway producer. Gerry promptly produced one of Michael's Broadway shows, a musical called *Honkytonk Nights*. Michael is an only child, just like me, so whenever he calls up, he says: "Hi, Jerry, this is your brother." Another Fire Island buddy, dear Jon Wilner, spent seven years of his life getting *Mack and Mabel* out of mothballs. If it weren't for Jon's perseverance, the London revival of that show would never have happened.

AND THEN, OF course, there were all those legendary ladies I came to know because of the roles I wrote for them.

There's no question that I love to write for women. To me, writing for a beautiful woman dressed in a glamorous gown and covered with jewels is a lot more exciting than writing for a man in a brown suit.

There was a regular parade of Dollys during the seven-year run of *Hello, Dolly!* and with one exception, I got to know them all. It was important to establish that personal relationship because each star had her own aura, something special that we would incorporate into the character of Dolly Levi so the part would become uniquely her own. I would always take my ladies out and get to know them while we were working on the score, and during their time in the show I would pay them court by visiting their dressing rooms and taking them out to dinner. In the summer I would invite a few special ladies to my place on Fire Island.

The one exception I mentioned was Martha Raye, who took over the role of Dolly when I was in the hospital with hepatitis. It was my job to work on the score with all the Dollys. I would rehearse them, change keys for them, do whatever I could to

With my best friend, Carol Dorian,
at the piano in 1966.

With Barnaby.

Swinging on my trapeze in my town house.

Bernadette Peters
and me.

Robert Preston and
Bernadette Peters
in *Mack and Mabel.*

Playing rehearsal piano in
1974 for our *Mack and
Mable* director Gower
Champion, Lisa Kirk,
and Robert Preston.

At the piece with
Joel Grey in 1979
for the first rehearsal
of *The Grand Tour*.

Lecturing at Musical Theater Works.
(*Photo: Rita Katz*)

The original *Jerry's Girls*, 1981.
Alix Korey, Leila Martin, Pauletta Pearson, and Evalyn Baron.

Carol Channing,
Leslie Uggams, and
Andrea McArdle
when *Jerry's Girls*
went on the road
in 1983.
(*Photo: Roger
Ressmeyer-Starlight*)

Andrea, Carol, and Leslie with our producer Zev Bufman
and me at the cast party for *Jerry's Girls*.
(*Photo: Bert and Richard Morgan Photographers*)

Marty Finkelstein and me.

My darling Sylvia Herscher has been one of
Jerry's Girls since 1960.

Arthur Laurents, Harvey Fierstein, and me at the
Colonial Theater in Boston in 1983, during the out-of-town
tryout of *La Cage aux Folles*. (*Photo: Waring Abbot*)

I am what I Am
I am my own special creation
_____   ovation
It's my world that I want to have a little pride in
_____ _____ and its not a place I have to hide in

George Hearn singing "I Am What I Am."
(*Photo: Martha Swope*)

Les Cagelles. (*Photo: Martha Swope*)

The *La Cage* chorus at the Palace Theater.
(*Photo: Martha Swope*)

At the big bash we
threw when *La Cage*
swept the 1984
Tony Awards.
(*Photo: Sam Siegal*)

Milton Berle and Sammy Davis, Jr., backstage at the
Palace Theater with Arthur Laurents, Gene Barry, and me.

In front of the Palace Theater and the Jerry Herman Way
sign that went up on 47th Street in 1985 when
La Cage played its 1500th performance.
(*Photo: Adam Newman Photography*)

With Michael Feinstein in 1993 at my star
on Hollywood Boulevard.

Me, Michael Feinstein, and Liza Minnelli.
(*Photo: Martha Swope Associates*)

Carol Dorian and me.
(*Photo: Julie Betts Testwide*)

My dear friend
Sheila Mack.

With my goddaughters, Jane Haspel
and 4-year-old Sarah.

Alice Borden and me.

With Karen Morrow and Lee Roy Reams, rehearsing our
nightclub act at Rainbow & Stars in 1989.
(*Photo: Aubrey Reuben*)

With the Hirschfeld drawing.

make them sound good and feel comfortable. So I was horrified that Miss Raye was in rehearsals and I was in the hospital, sick as a dog. I sent her a gorgeous telegram, apologizing because I was in the hospital and too sick to be with her, and for the opening I sent a magnificent bouquet of flowers to her dressing room.

I never heard a word back from her. Not a phone call in the hospital, not a little note thanking me for my gift, nothing. I thought that was strange, but I didn't brood about it because the doctors had agreed to let me out of the hospital so I could recuperate over the summer at my home on Fire Island.

When Sheila Mack got me out to Fire Island in a wheelchair it was a wonderful homecoming after all those months flat on my back, but I was still very weak and I had to stay in that wheelchair. After a few days, when I felt a little stronger, Sheila decided to wheel me down for lunch at this local restaurant called The Pavilion—and who should be sitting there having lunch but Martha Raye and these three gay guys!

I said, "Sheila, here is my star, and here I am in a wheelchair. What do I do?" And Sheila said, "Well, let's roll you over so you can introduce yourself."

So Sheila rolled me over, and I said, "Excuse me for interrupting, Miss Raye, but I'm Jerry Herman." Well, I got the coldest look you can imagine. Without even acknowledging my introduction, she said, "You've never been to see me." I pointed to my wheelchair and I said, "I just got out of the hospital. I have been there for months. Didn't you get my flowers and my wire? Didn't you know that I was very, very ill?"

She stared right at me and said, "Well, I thought you could have spared *one* evening."

After that, I *never* went to the St. James Theater to see her. And that's the end of my Martha Raye story.

* * *

W<small>ITH THAT ONE</small> exception, I had great fun with all the ladies, and some of them became very dear to me.

Carol Channing is my best friend and the love of my life. I think of my friendship with Carol as my reward for going through all that *sturm und drang* on *Hello, Dolly!* She is as close to me as any relative. She *is* my relative. She is my sister. A few years ago, when they asked me to be the Grand Marshal of the Gay Pride Parade in Los Angeles, Carol even became my Queen. The two of us shared the Grand Marshal honors, riding side by side in a white limousine at the head of the whole parade. We had the time of our lives.

Carol is also the only person who ever managed to get me into a disco, out on Fire Island. I wouldn't dance, though. Not even for her.

She is still full of beans, my darling Carol. She has a terrific sense of humor, and sometimes her humor can be very sly and subtle. She used to laugh at my little garden apartment on East Ninth Street. I could never see what was so funny about that place, which I had done up in a country decor with brick walls, barn doors, a rocking chair, and a big fireplace. To me, it was a wonderful place to work because it was very plain and nothing was in the way. But Carol said it reminded her of a monk's cell in a monastery because it was so tiny and cool and quiet, like one of those rooms where the monks copied the Bible. When she got on that subject she would call me Father Jerry.

In private, Carol is the exact opposite of Lorelei Lee. She's the perfect person to have at a dinner party because she is an exquisite conversationalist. We went out to dinner at Spago recently and Carol spent half the meal talking to Sharon Stone, who was at the next table. People who don't know Carol are always surprised how bright she is and how well versed she is in matters that have nothing to do with show business. She can talk international affairs and domestic politics and just about anything.

Charles Lowe, Carol's husband, is also family. He can be as big a character as Carol. I remember we did this big production of *Dolly!* in London and I flew over to make sure everything was all right. Charles called me up at the hotel and said, "I have a date for you for opening night."

I said to him, "Oh, please, Charles, my head is going to be in seventy-five different places on opening night. I am going to be a nervous wreck. The last thing I need to worry about is picking up some stranger and being a gentleman."

"Jerry, forgive me," Charles said. "But you have *got* to do this. This woman is the wife of the man who owns the *Daily Mail.*" Well, what could I do?

So on opening night I arrived in front of the Savoy. Standing right in front was my date—an enormous woman with these huge dimples, wearing a pink gown with tiers and tiers of pink tulle that went all the way down to the ground. She looked like a living lampshade. All I could think of was that scene in *Dolly!* when Ernestina dresses up in all her gaudy finery.

I almost told the cab driver to keep on going. Of course I didn't, but under my breath I said, "Charles Lowe, I'm gonna get you for this." Then I stepped out of the cab, gave my hand to my guest, and was as charming as I could be.

Lady Rothmere turned out to be a very lovely lady with a very bubbly personality. That was her nickname: Bubbles Rothmere. She almost smothered me in the taxicab with all that pink tulle, but I survived—and on the way to the theater I sold her my house for two million dollars.

I LOVED ALL the ladies, and some of them became my close personal friends. There was Betty Grable, who was an absolutely adorable woman, as simple and unpretentious as the girl next door. Betty was a warm human being and lovely to me personally. She was also a very sweet Dolly who brought this vulnerable quality to the role that was touching.

Betty Grable was also a very glamorous woman, the original pinup girl and an honest-to-God Hollywood legend. I mean, World War II would not have been World War II without Betty Grable. She used to come to my house on Fire Island, and when she sat around the pool sunbathing in her one-piece bathing suit, you could see that she still had those incredibly gorgeous legs.

That was such a thrill for this little Jewish boy from Jersey City, because when I was seven or eight years old I was in love with Betty Grable. She was the musical-comedy star of all those Coney Island and Wabash Avenue movies my mother used to let me go to see on Saturday afternoons. She was my big movie idol. I would send away to the movie studio for her autographed photographs, and I used to send her fan letters. And here was Betty Grable herself, standing in my kitchen in a *schmatta* doing the dishes and lounging around my pool with her hair dripping wet.

PEARL BAILEY WAS a big doll, a truly lovable lady. God knows what people would make of an all-black production of *Hello, Dolly!* if we did it today. It's probably entirely too politically incorrect to even discuss, but in 1967 it was right for the times. That whole company was enormously talented and we all had a good time.

Pearl was a story all by herself. She was hilarious, a very funny lady and a real hoot to work with. She was also a far more disciplined musician than I had expected. She sang every note and every lyric—she didn't change a thing. She would just add a little riff, a little shuffle, a little of the Pearl Bailey style that made the part of Dolly Levi entirely her own. And she always *asked* us if she could make these little style touches.

Pearl was kind of a rambunctious lady. The way she would throw these words around, you just had to laugh. I loved Pearl and she loved me, and she always wanted me to come into her dressing room. Now, the star dressing room at the St. James Theater is very tiny, not much bigger than a closet. There are far more luxurious accommodations upstairs, but every star wants *that* room, because it's on the first floor so you can do a quick change and run right back on stage.

I was going by the star dressing room one day when Pearl spotted me and said, "Jerry! Darling! Get in here quick—I have something to tell you."

I went in and right away she locked the door. Of course I am wondering what's so important that she would lock us into this little tiny room, because it was about ten minutes to eight and the star of the show was still in her slip.

Well, she started to tell me that the Lord had been on stage with her the night before. She told me this very seriously, because Pearl was always very serious about religion. I respected this about her, but I didn't know what to make of it when she started describing in great detail what the Lord was doing onstage. It seems that He was standing there in Mrs. Molloy's hat shop during the "Dancing" number, and He was doing the number along with the rest of the company.

A Jewish boy like me being told this story is funny enough to begin with. But I didn't want to offend Pearl, so I just stared at her, tongue-tied, during the entire story. By this time, she was late for her entrance, and the stage manager was banging down the door.

I don't remember what I finally said to Pearl to get her off this story and on the stage. But there was one thing I was *dying* to ask her—and to this day, I wish I'd had the guts. When she took my hand and told me that the Lord was on the stage with her, I wanted so desperately to say: "Did He know the lyrics?"

ANGELA LANSBURY WAS not only my Mame of Mames, she became my lifelong friend. The minute we met, Angela and I just connected.

Our friendship began with how I went out of my way to get her the lead in *Mame.* That show was such a triumph for her, and a real turning point in her career. She had come from another world entirely, playing character roles in Hollywood movies, and suddenly here she was, singing and dancing in a big stage musical, transformed into this glamorous Broadway star.

Mame really established me, too, so that show was important for both of us. The whole experience bonded us in an unusual way. We both watched each other having this incredible professional success, so we will always share this special link to the past.

The whole time Angela was in *Mame,* we would go out together and I would visit at the Dorset Hotel where she and her husband Peter had this lovely suite. Weekends, she would come out to my beach house where she could put her feet up and let her hair down. Those were wonderful, carefree weekends and we became quite a tight little group, Angela and Peter, my friends Sheila Mack and Jack Hutto.

We both have houses in Los Angeles now. Angie had a tragedy with an earlier house that burned up in a fire. She lost everything. I was heartbroken for her, and I was touched that the one thing that survived the fire was an antique gold bracelet with a diamond in the center that I gave her on the opening night of *Mame.* It suited her perfectly, and it is the one thing that wasn't lost in the fire because she was wearing it on her arm.

These days, I'm with Angela every minute, because we're working together on *Mrs. Santa Claus,* a new television musical I am writing for her. Whenever Angela and Peter come over for dinner, Sheila cooks and it's like old times.

NEXT TO Carol and Angela, the leading lady I became closest to was Ethel Merman. I adored that woman.

Ethel Merman was the first great lady I ever saw onstage. Her influence on me was immediate and tremendous—she just knocked me out. She made me fall in love with the musical theater. You'd think I would have been completely terrified of her, the way I was when I met Barbra Streisand, but that didn't happen and I can't explain why.

I met Merman when she showed up at my house at 50 West Tenth Street to hear the two songs I had originally written for her to sing in *Dolly!* I just opened the door and there she was—the queen of musical comedy on my doorstep.

There was every reason for me to have been scared to death of Ethel Merman, because she really was an awesome presence. She was tall and commanding and even when she was just talking naturally she had this *wild* voice. Even her jewelry was intimidating. She had a great jewel collection, and she came to my door in a very simple and stunning black crepe dress, wearing this huge pin that was like a sunburst of diamonds and rubies.

Plus, she had this reputation for being very strong-willed, very difficult to work with. It was well known that she didn't get along with a lot of people in the industry. I had heard all those stories, too.

And there was Ethel Merman on my doorstep. I really could have used a Valium, except we didn't have them in those days. But she didn't give me the chance to have a coronary. She swept into the house and up the stairs to my living room like some big, friendly puppy dog. She made herself right at home and she immediately started calling me "Jer." I guess she decided right away that she liked me.

We got to know each other that very first day and I think we both found something we liked—and needed—in each other. I can't explain it, it was just magical.

Merman was a no-nonsense Dolly. She played her tough and funny, but lovable underneath. And of course, she had the perfect voice for those songs, because I wrote some of them with her in mind. I remember how crushed I was when she originally turned down the show. It was so frustrating, because she wouldn't even listen to the songs.

She had explained her reasons very carefully to David Merrick at the time, and they were mainly that she was tired and wanted to rest. Ethel was famous for going straight from one show to the next without even blinking. Nobody went from show to show the way that Ethel Merman did. Nobody. But the lady was over sixty years old at the time, and she had just come off an exhausting run with *Gypsy*. I guess she really was getting tired. It wasn't until *Hello, Dolly!* was seven years into its Broadway run that Merman finally agreed to do the show. She said she would only do it for three months, but that engagement actually stretched into nine months.

Ethel called David Merrick herself for the job. "I hear that Jerry Herman wrote a couple of songs for me that were never used in the show," she said to Merrick. "That's right," David told her, "but we couldn't put them in the show because they are the kind of song that only Ethel Merman can sing." "I wanna hear 'em," she said to Merrick, who put her together with me. When I played the songs for for her she said, "I can handle 'em."

The opening night with Merman was in March of 1970 and it was such a thrill. She did her two new songs, "Love, Look In My Window" and "World, Take Me Back," just the way I dreamed of hearing them. After "World," I ran backstage and found her in the wings. She was ecstatic. She grabbed me by both arms and said, "I *told* you! I *told* you I could handle 'em!"

As we got to know each other, Merman let me more and more into her heart. I once found myself with her on a plane to the Coast. She thought we were going to appear on "The Merv Griffin Show" so she could sing the two songs I wrote for her in *Dolly!* Actually, it was a setup. I was really delivering her to *This Is Your Life.*

She told me many intimate things on that journey. Very private things about her relationship with her daughter. Very personal things about her feelings of loneliness and growing old. I realized that this woman must really like me to trust me with her secrets, because she didn't confide in many people. People only saw the steel facade she showed the world, but she let me see that behind the tough facade she was a big marsh-mallow.

So Ethel and I became great pals, and we stayed good friends for the rest of her life. She was a great lady, but I never felt I had to entertain her on some grand scale. She would come over and sometimes I just did some little dinner thing that I would cook with my friend Mark Reiner. Ethel always got a kick out of Ann Miller, and I remember one very small, pleasant dinner that I served for those two great ladies.

Besides being a good and loyal friend, Ethel Merman was one of the funniest human beings who ever walked on the planet. She was smart and she had this earthy humor and she was a riot when she told a story. She used to tell this absolutely hilarious, very raunchy story of being on a plane when a man had some difficulty getting his breath, and there was no doctor around. Well, when Merman got finished with him, this guy had superhuman lung power. He had *Merman* lung power.

When she was dying, her son called me up and said, "Ethel

would love to see you, if you feel you want to come." I was so touched to be one of the people she wanted to say goodbye to. I didn't know until that day the extent of her affection for me.

I am glad that we were able to say goodbye, but I hate to think of her the way she was that day, propped up in bed and looking so fragile. It was just heartbreaking. This was a lady who was so alive, so much bigger than life that you never, ever wanted to see her incapacitated. *La Cage* had just opened and she was so happy for my success, because she was one of the few people who really knew what those years had been like for me. I was so proud to bring her the album and put it on her bed, and I am so happy that she heard it before she died.

BETWEEN ALL THE Dollys and all the Mames, I became pals with some of the most glamorous women in the world—ladies like Dorothy Lamour, Ginger Rogers, Celeste Holm, Janis Paige, Jayne Morgan, and Lisa Kirk. I had a special relationship with Lisa, who played Lottie in *Mack and Mabel*. The two of us love to cook, so she would come over and cook dinner with me, and then we'd sit around and talk for hours.

There were some stunning Mames who came after Angela. Janis Paige was frankly too young for the part, but she was one of the most likable ladies on stage and our audiences were crazy about her. Jayne Morgan was a big singer with a magnificent voice that absolutely thrilled me. Celeste Holm acted the hell out of Mame. She had a lovely voice and a sunniness about her that made her irresistible, so we became great pals.

Ann Miller was the last of the Broadway Mames. She was very warm and funny and we added a special tap routine for her in "That's How Young I Feel" that stopped the show. Annie is a good sport and we became quite friendly. We always catch up when we run into each other at opening nights.

I also had the incredible experience of working with Susan

Hayward, who played Mame in Las Vegas. When she came to my house so I could teach her the score, she took my breath away. With that sweetheart face of hers, she was movie-star gorgeous. You could tell she knew how to wear clothes just by the way she had this cashmere sweater draped casually over her shoulders. I have met many handsome and stylish women in my day; but Susan Hayward and Lana Turner were the most beautiful women I ever saw in my life.

Of all the Dollys, the biggest surprise was Phyllis Diller. I was a little afraid that we were going to get a wild, crazed Dolly, because Phyllis Diller is one of the funniest women who was ever born. She could have made funny faces or slipped in a few of her raunchy stories, but she didn't. She was absolutely professional and she played it simply and honestly—no gimmicks. She was a doll.

AND THEN THERE was Mary Martin, who was the most unpretentious person you'd ever want to meet. All she wanted to do was work on her needlepoint and live a quiet life with her husband Richard Halliday in this little enclave they had in the jungles of Brazil.

We wanted Mary to do *Mame*, so Bobby Fryer and I went all the way down to Brazil to talk to her. The only way to get to the secluded place where she and Richard lived was by flying in on these little planes and then taking a jeep that shook your bones and rattled your kidneys.

Richard and Mary loved the whole rural life, which was pretty primitive by most people's standards. There was no heat and no regular electricity. I think they had generators. There was no television. Water had to be boiled. It was real pioneer living. Bobby Fryer and I—two very spoiled city boys—went down and had a hysterical time.

We absolutely hated it. But we loved it because it was such a weird, funny experience. The cabins for visitors were like little motel units, with screens all around. The first night we were there, Mary showed us to our cabin and stood in the doorway.

"Don't be disturbed if you hear these whooshing sounds during the night," she told us. "We have bats." And then she waved her hand and said "Goodnight!" so sweetly.

Bobby was in the bed right across the room from me, but he didn't say a word. Neither did I. We both turned out our lamps and lay absolutely still. And then, all of a sudden, something went "Whoooosh" and flew right into one of the screen windows.

Bobby started giggling, and he has a giggle that could crack me up in the middle of a funeral. After we both stopped laughing, it was quiet again—until another bat went "Whoosh" and slammed into the screen. That got us started again. We were laughing too hard to talk, but whenever it got really quiet one of us would stick his head up and whisper: "Whoosh." All night long, between the bats going "Whoosh," and Bobby and me whooshing each other, I don't think I got ten minutes' sleep.

This remote compound where Richard and Mary lived was somewhere up the Amazon, I don't know exactly where, and I don't want to think about what went on there. It wasn't just the bats. There were snakes all over the place and these things in the trees that used to scream at us. I remember saying to Bobby, "Well, after I take my life in my hands, she *better* do this show."

Mary Martin never did do *Mame*. But she became one of the most important of all my Dollys when she went over to Vietnam in *Hello, Dolly!* to entertain the troops. That was a spectacular occasion, and there is a magnificent *Life* magazine cover photo of Mary, standing on the runway in front of a sea of soldiers and smiling that radiant smile of hers. She really was an adorable lady—cute and warm and very loving. But at that stage in her life Mary wouldn't commit to a show for any kind of a run. She said the same thing that Merman said, that after all those years of performing she wanted to live a normal life—if you can call living in the Amazon jungle a normal life.

What the two of them did out there in this jungle, I never did find out. Richard had horses and he was always riding. Mary used to read and do her needlepoint. They really enjoyed the solitude. Me, I would have gone stark raving mad. Bobby and I finally cooked up some story and we escaped to civilization via Rio.

I FOUND MARY Martin in the jungle and I found Ethel Merman on my doorstep, but you never know where you're going to find the ladies who are going to become important in your life. Florence Lacey was introduced to me at a Christmas party at Rock Hudson's house. This is the lady who did my Hollywood Bowl show and who appeared with me when I did my New York act at Rainbow and Stars. I consider Florence one of the best interpreters of my music.

Rock was a good friend, and when he came over to me at this Christmas party he said, "Stay there. Don't move. You have got to meet this girl." And then he brought over this gorgeous creature with deep blue eyes and lovely long hair and this absolutely exquisite face. She was so ravishing I was dazzled.

Rock took one look at my face and he laughed. "Her name is Florence," he said. "She sings, too." And then he asked us to do something together.

Well, I love to accompany. I am a much better accompanist than I am a pianist. It's a different art. You don't play the melody. You are the whole orchestra with two hands. I love that.

So I asked this beautiful girl what she wanted to sing and she said "Can't Help Lovin' That Man." I loved that she knew the verse. Rock didn't make any announcement, and we didn't even take a minute to rehearse. We just *did* it. And when Florence opened her mouth and this exquisite voice came out, all two hundred people at this Christmas party stopped what they were doing and turned around. It was like everybody stopped breathing.

I didn't know what Florence was going to do and she didn't know what I was going to do, but it didn't matter. We were like one soul. It was a great moment and the place went wild. So then we *really* flattened them out with this very obscure song from *Miss Liberty* called "I Don't Want Him, You Can Have Him."

When it was over, Florence and I hugged each other and became fast, permanent friends. I hired her on the spot to play Mrs. Molloy in the Houston Grand Opera production of *Dolly!*. For the first time, the young lovers were beautiful, they were romantic—and they sang their asses off.

JUST THINKING ABOUT all these ladies makes me realize how lucky I have been. Can you imagine being able to say that you worked with Lucille Ball and Barbara Streisand and Susan Hayward and on and on and on?

You know, these are *real people* underneath all the wigs and the eyelashes and the stage makeup. It isn't the big star that you become friends with—it's the lady underneath. I can't say what these women saw in me, but what I found in them was humor, warmth, and sincerity.

These are people with a world to talk about and to share, and I am grateful that they chose to share it with me. There is one thing about me that probably makes it easy for ladies like this to have me in their lives—they know that I understand the perils of celebrity. I've not only worked with these women,

I've also been out with them in public. I know what it feels like to be arm in arm with Ethel Merman when people would mob her in the streets. Some of that is fun, but not a constant lifetime of it. That kind of celebrity becomes very oppressive. Most of these big stars would do anything for a quiet evening away from all that madness.

I think what they see in me is somebody who's basically shy and doesn't want that kind of public attention. They can feel comfortable with me. I'm somebody they can talk show business with, but who still lets them be themselves. They know that I don't expect them to act like a star and that I'm not going to drag them around and show them off. I'm perfectly happy if they come to my house in jeans and we sit on the floor and eat sandwiches and laugh. We can have fun without some big glamorous hoo-hah.

I have had a wonderful lifetime of working with remarkable women, and it makes me sad that so many of the great ladies I have known are gone. Ethel and Mary and Pearl and Betty and Ginger are gone, all of them. I've been thinking that, in a way, the era of my life is also the era of the great ladies of the American musical.

I hate to say it, but that era may be over for the theater, too. Nobody's writing those kind of shows anymore—not for the great ladies of musical theater. And if we did create those shows again, would Barbra Streisand or Liza Minnelli do them on the stage? I doubt it. It probably sounds too harsh to say that an entire era is over, but certainly it's the end of a cycle. I am sorry that so many people had to miss it, but speaking for myself, the era of the great ladies was a glorious time in the American theater.

ELEVEN

"I Don't Want to Know"

UP UNTIL *MAME*, I had just had a few passing romantic relationships, but nothing serious or long-lasting. Right after *Mame* opened and was such a huge success, I began a three-year friendship with a lovely man who owned a restaurant in St. Thomas.

Sheila Mack and I had gone down to the Virgin Islands to celebrate. We were supposed to be on vacation relaxing, but Sheila said, "I have a friend who owns a restaurant down here. We have got to visit him." I said to myself, "Oh, my God, I'll be bored to death." So I asked Sheila, "Do I really have to go with you?" Sheila said, "Oh, please! I haven't seen this man in years and I'll be much more comfortable with you." So I said I'd go, but I wasn't happy.

I remember we had to climb this endless flight of stairs to the restaurant. And there at the top of the stairs was this absolutely gorgeous, suntanned man with dark hair and the most amazing blue eyes. I said, "Oh, my God! *That's* your friend?" Sheila didn't get it. We barely sat down before she started making excuses so we could leave. She thought I was bored, so she said, "Well, George, it was great seeing you, but Jerry and I have these plans . . ."

"No, we don't," I said. "We have all the time in the world, George. What are you doing this afternoon?"

Well, it turned out that we had a three-year relationship. It was a little difficult to maintain, because I lived in New York and he lived in St. Thomas. But the airport scenes were very exciting.

That was my first serious relationship and it was lovely. One of the nice things about the times we had together was that George loved my piano-playing, so I was always playing for him. Once, for his birthday, I took myself into a professional recording studio, sat myself down at the piano, and played all his favorite songs. The studio made a disc for me and put it in a blank album cover. When I brought the album home, I said to Sheila, "Come on, we are going to turn this place into an arts and crafts studio."

And that's what we did. We used these gorgeous materials to make a cover for the album, and then in bright blue letters— the color of his eyes—we spelled out: *Jerry Plays for GEORGE.*" It was a professional-looking album and visually very stunning. George nearly fainted when he got it in the mail on his birthday.

I was a very romantic lover, and this was a very romantic time for me.

Success also gave me the confidence to assert my own taste when it was time to choose my next project.

When I was a student at the University of Miami, I played the deaf mute in Jean Giraudoux's *The Madwoman of Chaillot*, which was how I happened to fall in love with that play. It is a delicate piece of work about an old woman considered by most people to be mad, but who singlehandedly stops a group of greedy, unscrupulous businessmen from destroying Paris.

I thought this piece was very lyrical and very musical and I always had it in mind to do a musicalization of the play. This seemed like the perfect time, because I wanted to do something that was a real departure from *Dolly!* and *Mame*. What could be more different and daring than a musical about an eighty-year-old madwoman who lives in a sewer?

I went to Alexander H. Cohen, because I knew Alex from writing special material for his Tony Award shows. Alex and his wife, Hildy Parks, are probably the most loyal people in the business and I love that about them.

I told Alex that my idea was a little offbeat, but he thought it was fascinating—so I had a producer. Then I went to Lawrence and Lee, who love to work on challenging literary material, and they were excited—so I had my book writers. And then I sat down and got to work on what would become *Dear World*.

I HAD A terrific time writing the score. I deliberately stayed away from the show-biz sound and went for a sound that was much more legitimate, even classical. In fact, this one piece called "The Tea Party," which has three separate melodies layered on top of one another, could have come straight out of classical opera. I wasn't writing art songs to be precious; it just seemed appropriate for this material, which is essentially a philosophical fairytale.

I loved working with Lawrence and Lee again, and getting to know the internal workings of Giraudoux's play was a kind of enchantment. Everything felt so right when I was writing this score, which I think is of a higher caliber than either *Dolly!* or *Mame*. It's more mature, it's more classical, it's more inventive, it's more daring.

The score is loaded with all kinds of challenging stuff. Singers find "I Don't Want to Know" exciting to work with because it builds and builds in emotion like a Jacques Brel song. Angela used to stop the show every night with that song, and when Liza sang it in her Carnegie Hall concert she brought the house down.

"And I Was Beautiful" invites us all to remember a time in our lives when we were young and happy and beautiful because someone loved us. Angela sang it propped up in this cobwebby bed, lost in reverie that the young man lying by her side was her first, lost love. That was an exquisite moment and Angela was achingly beautiful.

I wanted people to listen to that song and to be touched by the loneliness and the vulnerability of that woman. If you want that kind of emotion, you have to write something that is the very essence of simplicity, a song that doesn't have a false note or an excessive word anywhere.

Simplicity is the hardest thing to achieve in a song. Ideally, music and lyric should be indelibly interlocked.

> "He stood and looked at me
> And I was beautiful
> For it was beautiful
> How he believed in me
> His love was strong enough
> To make me anything
> So I was ev'rything
> He wanted me to be
> But then he walked away
> And took my smile with him
> And now the years blur by
> But ev'ry now and then
> I stop and think of him
> And how he looked at me
> And all at once
> I'm beautiful again."

I love that song.

Dear World also makes me proud because there is such variety to the work. The songs go from art pieces like "The Tea Party" to tender ballads like "Kiss Her Now." Some of the things in that score are very subtle—they can really fool you.

"The Spring of Next Year," for instance, sounds like a pretty waltz straight out of *Gigi* or *Blossom Time*. But if you listen, there is real irony in the lyrics, because the characters who are singing this sweeping melody are hardened villains, and the spring air that they are singing about is actually pollution.

> "There will be a sweet taste in the air
> From industrial waste in the air
> And your eyelids will smart from the sting of
> The smog in the spring of
> Next year
> There will be a black slick on the Seine
> And the sludge will be thick on the Seine
> And your eardrums will sting from the ring of
> The axe in the spring of
> Next year
> Ah, the apple trees blooming
> As they're crushed into pulp
> There'll be smokestacks consuming
> Each available gulp
> That's inhalable
> But the moment most thrilling begins
> When the pneumatic drilling begins
> It's a song that all Paris will sing
> In the bountiful spring
> Of next year."

Can you imagine how much fun I had writing that?

ONE OF THE trickiest songs I wrote for *Dear World*—"Through the Bottom of the Glass"—never even made it into the show.

213

It had endless lyric variations on the language of liquor, especially on the lyrical names of liqueurs like anisette and Char-
treuse. The madwoman peered through a brandy snifter and
saw the world in that distorted image.

"What a fascinating view
Through the bottom of the glass
A December afternoon looks particularly well
When you watch it drift along through some sunny muscatel
It's the middle of July
Through the bottom of the glass
What a fascinating view
Through the facets in the ice
The beggars and the rogues
That we socially condemn
Are the court of Antoinette
Through the prism of the stem
So I watched them saunter by
Through the bottom of the glass . . .
So I simply let life pass
Through the rose of the rosé
Through the amber of the rum
Through an endless pousse café
Through the bottom of the glass."

The funny thing about that song was that I hadn't the vaguest
idea what those drinks actually tasted like. Only my friends and
people who have worked with me can appreciate the little joke
about that song, because they know what a teetotaler I am.

My mother and father kept a huge, well-stocked bar in the
party room in our basement where their friends used to come
to dance. So alcohol was very much a part of my growing up,
just like coffee, which my father and grandmother drank all
day long. I just never liked the stuff, so I never touched it.

I was such a notorious tea drinker that it became a running

joke in the theater. The stage manager on a show is the person who usually handles all the food and drink orders for the cast and crew. On my shows, the guy would come back from the deli and yell, "Coffee break: 32 doughnuts, 32 bagels, 64 coffees—and one tea!"

It was the same way when we went out to eat. The whole table would order booze—and a ginger ale for Jerry. But I never felt that being a non-drinker set me apart from people, because I have the kind of personality that lets me go along with whatever the general mood is. I have such fun at a party that half the time people don't even realize I am totally sober. I actually like it when people get a little high and act silly, because I can let out my own silliness. Even at a drunken party, I am totally comfortable.

Drugs are another thing. When I was with Marty, the dear friend I spent many years of my life with, I tried recreational drugs just like everybody else. Maybe once a month we would have a crazy evening taking a little of this, a little of that. At the time, everybody was doing it because it was the thing to do. But that's where it stopped.

I would never make drugs a part of my life because I came to see drugs as destructive to good work. I have watched too many people I respected and admired in the theater go through terribly destructive character changes because of drugs. I also watched their work suffer, which was tragic.

That's what *really* scared me about drugs. I never wanted to write a lousy song that I stupidly thought was brilliant because I had written it when I was high. For that reason, I have never in my life written a single piece of music under the influence of anything—not even aspirin.

EACH ONE OF those songs in *Dear World* had something that made it challenging. The orchestration that I originally had in mind for this offbeat score was something quite simple. I was picturing a small group of street musicians playing a concertina and a flute, maybe a fiddle. That would be the basic sound of the orchestra, enhanced by a few more instruments in the pit.

I didn't want to get any more elaborate than that, because this was going to be an elegant little chamber piece for a singing ensemble of no more than a dozen performers. I didn't want any big chorus sing-songs and I didn't want any big dance numbers. What I was after was the unusual look and the strange, haunting sound of a little Parisian street band.

I'm happy to say that that's exactly the way the show will someday be done in a new, rewritten version called *The Madwoman*. Unfortunately for the show, that's exactly the way that *Dear World* was *not* done on Broadway in 1969. I can't say exactly how it happened, but things just got completely out of hand.

I THINK IT all started when the producer called up to tell me that he had booked the Mark Hellinger Theater.

"The *Hellinger*?" I said. "That great big theater for this little art musical with these odd orchestrations and with eleven people in the whole cast?" But as Alex pointed out, it was a real coup to get a desirable house like the Hellinger. This was back in the days when Broadway had a booking jam. There were so many shows coming in, you had to stand in line to get a decent theater. The Hellinger was also well located, which made it the kind of theater where you could make real money if you had a hit.

From that moment, everything turned around and started going in a different direction.

In one sense I was pleased, because the Hellinger is a gorgeous theater and I was proud to have my little show in such a splendid setting. But because the Hellinger is also a *huge* theater, we had to fill the place with sound. And once you have a bigger sound, you need more elaborate orchestrations. Phil Lang gave the score a lush sound that was absolutely beautiful, and there's no question that it was a *big* beautiful sound.

That expansive sound translated into more instruments, more musicians, more singers, more of everything. The next thing you knew, we had these elegant sets and lavish costumes, and all the rest of it. Maybe the last straw was when we got a dancing chorus that looked like the chorus line in *Mame*.

Part of me still wants to blame the theater for the failure of *Dear World*. Who knows? Maybe everything might have turned out differently if we had booked a smaller, more intimate house like the Golden. But to tell the truth, I think the whole production was much too overblown for the delicacy of the material.

It was like nothing could stop this thing. The bigger it got, the more changes we had to make in the original idea. At some point, we realized that we couldn't get some character actress out of mothballs to play the lead in this big musical—we needed a star.

It was my idea to ask Angela Lansbury. "Angela is the best actress in the world," I told Alex, "and I think she would be brilliant." Alex went crazy over the idea, so I invited Angela to my house at the beach and played some of the songs for her. "I would love to do this," she told me. "It's a wonderful acting challenge."

Angela gave a luminous performance as the Madwoman. She won her second Tony Award for that performance, and she deserved it. But putting a star in the role was another kind of mistake, because it sent out the wrong message about the show. Angela's fans went to the show expecting to see her in a glamorous role. The last thing they expected to see was that lovely, elegant lady dressed in rags, with ugly wrinkles painted on her face—playing a crazy old lady who lives in a sewer.

People were very disappointed. Some of them actually came up to me and said, "Did you *have* to make her look like *that?*"

ONE MISTAKE LED to another.

Maybe the biggest problem was that we went through three different directors. We started out working with Lucia Victor, who had been Gower Champion's assistant on *Dolly!*. I was crazy about Lucia, but she was not an experienced director for a big Broadway show like this one had turned into.

We switched to the English director Peter Glenville when we were out of town in Boston. Peter worked with Angela and restaged certain things, and I adored everything he did. He was a gifted director and he took a very stylish approach that was both cerebral and emotional, which was the proper style for this sort of material.

I always felt that if Peter Glenville had finished the show we would have had something totally different. But he had come in for only a short period of time as a personal favor to Angela. He had other projects and couldn't stay.

At this point we got Joe Layton, who finished the project in an entirely different style. Joe was a wonderful stager and choreographer, but as a director he was much showier and more dance-oriented. What he brought to our show was more entertainment value, which was not what it needed.

IT NEVER FAILS. You work and work for months and months and when you're in the rehearsal studio you think you have achieved perfection. But only the audience can tell you the truth. In our case, we kept fooling ourselves that the problems were getting solved. But the minute we stood the show up in front of the out-of-town audience, we knew we were in serious trouble.

The Boston critics knew it, too, because the opening night reviews were mixed to negative. So the next morning, we all sat down very soberly—Alex, Angela, Lawrence and Lee, and me—and we talked about changes. Alex had to deal with our director troubles. Lawrence and Lee had to cut the fat and get rid of all the redundant material. My job was to write two new songs.

The first one, "A Sensible Woman," went in for a couple of days, but never made it into the show. I don't remember exactly why, because I took it out of the trunk recently and I liked it a lot. It's an interesting piece of work and maybe I'll do something with it someday.

The other hotel-room song, "I Don't Want to Know," is one of my favorite pieces.

I wrote that song very quickly, because it was the key piece that had been missing all along from the show—but which I hadn't realized until then. It is one of my "statement" songs like "I Am What I Am" and "Before the Parade Passes By." It's the Madwoman's statement that she is angry with the misery and the ugliness and the cruelty in the world, and she is not going to put up with it any more.

I think it is a very beautiful song, but it is also very fierce. The music, which is in waltz time, gets faster and wilder as the emotion builds.

> "If music is no longer lovely
> If laughter is no longer lilting
> If lovers are no longer loving
> Then I don't want to know
> If summer is no longer carefree
> If children are no longer singing
> If people are no longer happy
> Then I don't want to know
> Let me hide ev'ry truth from my eyes
> With the back of my hand

> Let me live in a world full of lies
> With my head in the sand
> For my memories all are exciting
> My memories all are enchanted
> My memories burn in my head
> With a steady glow
> So if, my friends, if love is dead
> I don't want to know."

Angela just adored that song. It was a great musical moment for her. She stood alone on the stage when she sang it, and the lighting behind her turned from the pale blue of a Paris sky to a deep red sunset that looked like fire. When she hit the last chords of the second chorus, the sky was throbbing and there she was, standing alone and majestic in Freddie Wittop's magnificent rags.

At the Hellinger, the ovations were such a *roar*, you could hear them outside the theater. Wherever I was, whatever I was doing, I used to rush into the theater and stand at the back of the house for that moment. It was breathtaking. I think that song won Angela her Tony Award.

BY THE TIME *Dear World* opened in New York, it was in much better shape than it was in Boston. But we still wound up with all three directorial styles on the stage. Some of the performers were working in our latest style, but others were still working in the earlier styles. Peter Glenville's influence was still on Angela, and our ingenue, who came to us late, was entirely directed by Joe Layton.

Opening night in New York was not a happy experience for any of us. It was especially sad for me, because the show had been my idea and I felt responsible for giving up my original concept. Other people may have been technically responsible for choosing the wrong theater and the wrong style and for allowing the show to get so big and clumsy. But those mistakes were my fault, too. I could have said: "Hey, wait a minute, everybody! This is not what I set out to do. Let's go back and find that original, wonderful idea that we lost."

But of course I never said that. I didn't want to be the person who pushed himself ahead of the team like that. It wasn't that I didn't trust my judgment. But you are supposed to be cooperative and collaborative in the theater, and I wanted more than anything to be a good collaborator. I wanted to be a nice guy.

So I didn't speak up, and partly because of me people were deeply disappointed in *Dear World*. The audience seemed to feel that we had misled them about this show. Which is true, in a way, if you look at the full-page ad that we took out in The New York *Times*. That picture of Angela was the glamor photo of all time. She had this white fur draped around her nude shoulders and she wore her hair in this sensational upswept hairdo. She looked like a glam movie star in one of those MGM studio shots.

The names on that ad were the same names from *Mame*— Angela Lansbury, Jerry Herman, Lawrence and Lee—so naturally, ninety-five percent of the people who responded to that ad thought they were getting another big, glamorous show like *Mame*. When they found themselves at this odd little French fairytale, I think they were terribly confused.

THE CRITICS WERE not only confused, they were furious. Something about the entire venture seemed to rub them the wrong way. It was as if they were personally offended by *Dear World*.

One thing they really hated us for was the forty-four previews. That really irritates critics, long preview periods.

They think the show is trying to sneak in without getting reviewed.

The truth is, we really needed the time to work on the show. But working in New York is like being in a fishbowl. It is no atmosphere to work in because the word about a show's problems filters through the industry like water through a sieve. Twelve hours after your first preview you start getting calls. The whole industry has formulated its opinion of the show before the critics even arrive.

Not only did the critics dismiss the entire show, but for the first time in my life, I got personal notices that were very cruel. I was stunned.

To be fair, I should say that some of the reviewers were kind, and that Walter Kerr, in particular, was very generous about the score. But you tend to forget the good things when you've been hurt, and what I remember are the really stinging notices. The review in *Time* magazine will stay in my head forever, because it said that the score was a total zero. Now, it's one thing to dislike this song or that song, or even the basic sound—but how can you dismiss an entire score with three or four pieces of work that I consider my finest?

I also felt terrible for Angela, who was deeply disappointed. It helped that she won a Tony Award, and that people all said that she gave a beautiful performance. But the experience was not a happy one for Angie. She had just come from *Mame*. She had been the toast of New York, and this was supposed to be her glory time. Instead, she was in a show that wasn't working.

Angela also didn't like playing an old woman. She had played old women in Hollywood until we came along and turned her into this brand-new, glamorous creature. She loved it, all of it. She loved wearing gorgeous costumes and kicking her legs higher than all the chorus kids. And why shouldn't she? She had earned it.

Now, all of a sudden, this stunning woman was on a New

York stage dressed in rags and wearing wild makeup that made her look like Bette Davis's crazy grandmother.

My own experience made me seriously mistrust the professional judgment of critics. On a personal level, it also made me wonder if there was something else behind the hurtful tone of the notices. It seemed to me that the reviewers were very cruel—too cruel—to me. Maybe I had enjoyed too much success and they thought they had to bring me down. I don't know. I do know that I am very proud of that score and I am very glad I wrote it because it broadened me as a writer.

The sad thing for me was that this difficult experience made me take a few steps backward into my reclusive past, when I had been so isolated that I was practically living like a hermit. For a while, I just didn't want to go out of the house and have to face everybody. I felt that I had failed myself and let everybody down.

It wasn't a *totally* terrible time. I had my good friends, and I had a lovely romance with Joe Masiell, who had played a small part in *Dear World*. That was a rare thing for me, to have a relationship with someone in one of my shows. It was kind of a taboo thing with me. I never thought it was a good idea and usually stayed away from it, because I didn't want the other kids to think I was giving someone preferential treatment.

But it happened. We met and we liked each other and we had a very nice time. Joe was the nicest, sweetest guy, and for about a year we had good times and we laughed a lot.

Dear World ran for about six months and I tried to put up a good front. But I have to admit that it wasn't as much fun to visit the Mark Hellinger Theater as it had been to visit the Winter Garden and the St. James. Nobody was angry with anybody, but you could feel the terrible disappointment. That company thought they would be with this show for years. The kids in the chorus thought they would never have to look for another job.

My problem was, I was spoiled. I thought you just wrote a musical and it ran for seven years. I had just sailed through an entire decade in which I could do no wrong, only to enter an entire decade in which I could do nothing right. After writing three hits in a row, in the 1970s I would write three musicals that were total failures. Talk about an emotional roller coaster!

I don't want to shy away from the word *failure,* because that's exactly what it was. But *total* isn't the right word at all, because two of those shows, *Dear World* and *Mack and Mabel,* became cult classics.

An album of *Dear World* was released on the Columbia label and is still selling quite well, so that score found a small cult of people who still love it. A lot of musicians, especially, have written me over the years to say nice things about the music. Even back then, when the show was still running, I could see that people were finding the material and using it in their nightclub acts. That helped me to feel a little better about my failure.

Later on, *Mack and Mabel* would become an even bigger cult favorite than *Dear World.* Even now, when I try to tell someone that *Mack and Mabel* was a failure, they look at me as if I were raving mad. Today, that score is perceived as an extraordinary piece of work. But in its day, it too was a big flop.

TWELVE

"Just Go to the Movies"

AFTER THE FAILURE of *Dear World,* I said to myself: "What do I do now? Do I sulk? Do I stamp my feet and say that I'm never going to write another show because the critics didn't acknowledge my wonderful work?"

My answer to myself was: "No, I am going to start looking for material for a new project."

Meanwhile, life wasn't all that tough—not when you have three musicals playing simultaneously on Broadway. During those months that *Dear World* was running, I had a marvelous time running from show to show. There were nights when I would start at *Dear World* so I could see Angela sing "I Don't Want to Know." After going backstage to kiss everybody, I would dash from the Mark Hellinger to the Winter Garden to catch the end of Act One of *Mame.* I would spend intermission gossipping in the dressing rooms before strolling down Broadway to Forty-fourth Street, where I would stop in at the St. James in time to watch the "Hello, Dolly" number stop the show. And then after the show I would go out with one of my ladies.

That was a heady time for me. But even though I was having the time of my life, I was still looking for my next project.

One day, a man named Leonard Spigelgass invited me out to lunch. "I have this wonderful idea for a musical about Mack Sennett and Mabel Normand," he told me. "I would love to tell you about it." I had only vaguely heard about this old-time Hollywood producer and the actress who starred in his silent pictures, but once Leonard started talking about these two people I could see what a great idea this was for a musical.

The story is set in early Hollywood, so it had the fun of the Keystone Kops and bathing beauties at the beach and all that glorious madness that Mack Sennett invented. I immediately got all excited about trying to create the sound of this particular period. The most appealing thing to me, though, was the distinctive romance between this big Hollywood producer and the actress he fell in love with. It was a very tough romance and these were two fascinating people.

Leonard Spigelgass was a very decent man. Shortly after we had our lunch, he called me up and said, "Jerry, I hate to do this to you. I was the one who got you all excited about this project, and now I have to tell you that my head is not really in it right now because I am writing a book. But I still love the idea and I want you to do it. If you can give me a little piece of the total work, I want you to go ahead and find your own book writer."

So I went to my brother, which is how I thought of Michael Stewart. We had such a special relationship, the two of us. Our styles were very similar and because of the way we wrote together, we were good for each other. I recently told someone that if Michael Stewart had not died so young, we would have three shows running on Broadway right now.

Anyway, I went to Mike and I said, "I have found our new musical. You are going to love it." And he did. All I had to do was describe the idea and he said, "Let's meet on Monday morning and get to work."

* * *

MACK AND MABEL was pure fun for me. "Movies Were Movies" was exactly the sound of the music they used to play in movie theaters for silent pictures. That sound gave me a new direction and put me on fresh musical ground. I also had a great time writing "Hundreds of Girls" for the Mack Sennett bathing beauties. You can imagine my delight, writing lyrics like:

> "What gives a man
> Power and punch
> Tina for breakfast
> And Lena for lunch
> Having hundreds and hundreds of girls
> I'll fill the screen
> With Jan and Jane and Joan and Janet and Jean
> I'll pull the greatest stunt this business has seen
> 'Till every fella' from Duluth to Atlanta sees
> All of his fantasies
> Sinner or saint, schoolgirl or queen
> One girl is boring and two are obscene
> Give 'em hundreds and hundreds of girls!"

But the whole score *really* burst into bloom for me when I studied the romance between Mack and his Mabel.

Here was a man who truly loved this woman but who was never able to tell her so. He wasn't able to say, very simply: "I love you, kid." He couldn't do that because he was an introspective kind of guy who was too obsessive about his moviemaking. At the same time, he really *wanted* her to know that he loved her. And because she was so insecure, Mabel really *needed* to hear him say it.

I used to walk up and down the streets of New York for hours, thinking about this impossible relationship. One day when I was walking along, thinking out loud, I came up with these lines in Mack Sennett's gruff voice. The lines were: "I won't send roses, or hold the door / I won't remember what dress you wore." That was his style. That was his very voice.

Well, I raced through the streets like a nut and ran home to put those lines on the piano. I started playing around with five musical notes, and pretty soon they melted into my first line, and the song started to come together.

I must have played that little tune for weeks. I could not stop playing the beginning of that song. But that was all I had—the beginning. I didn't have any middle and I didn't have my caboose. I didn't even have a complete melody.

But I knew what I wanted Mack to say—which was basically, "Stay away, kid." So I jumped to the last line. Suddenly, this same gruff voice comes out and says, "I won't send roses—and roses suit you so."

That line was so perfect, I lost my mind. It's a hell of a thing to say to a girl, because it's so tough. But it is also very romantic, and it is exactly what Mabel wants to hear. That line still gives me shivers. I think it says more about those two people than anything in the whole show.

> "I won't send roses
> Or hold the door
> I won't remember
> Which dress you wore
> My heart is too much in control
> The lack of romance in my soul
> Will turn you gray, kid
> So stay away, kid
> Forget my shoulder
> When you're in need
> Forgetting birthdays
> Is guaranteed
> And should I love you
> You would be

>The last to know
>I won't send roses
>And roses suit you so."

I am just as proud of Mabel's response, which is set to the same melody and is just as unsentimental. Bernadette Peters used to sing it with her head high and cocky: "So who wants chocolates? They'd make me fat." But when she sang her last line—"So who needs roses / That didn't come from him"— that "him" was so tender and so sad, she always broke my heart. I always had to go off somewhere to recover.

That song is what the show is all about, which is the unlikely romantic love story of two opposites. That was a great love story. It was certainly the best love story I ever wrote about.

I DON'T PICK characters because I feel some personal affinity for them. Maybe I pick some of them because they are *not* me.

Mack Sennett was *definitely* not me, and yet he was one of the most fascinating characters in the world. I found something touching in the man, but I didn't admire him. He neglected Mabel and caused her to get involved in drugs. The person who did that was not my kind of hero.

I did very much admire what Mack did for Mabel in the end, when she was down and out. He hocked his studio for her. Nobody in Hollywood would hire her anymore because she was taking drugs, so Mack bankrupted himself to finance this serious movie called *Molly* for her to star in. He knew the movie would never be released, but he made it anyway, to show her that she was still a star and still had a career. That was such a loving thing to do, and it was even more meaningful because Mack Sennett deliberately went broke to make that gesture of love to Mabel Normand.

I just loved *Mack and Mabel*. There was so much that was

right about that play. The production got a lot of it right, too. Robert Preston was a wonderful Mack Sennett, very strong and manly, and Bernadette Peters was absolutely exquisite as Mabel. She was funny, vulnerable, and also very feisty. Her "Time Heals Everything" was classic.

> "Time heals everything
> Tuesday, Thursday
> Time heals everything
> April, August
> If I'm patient, the break will mend
> And one fine morning the hurt will end
> So make the moments fly
> Autumn, winter
> I'll forget you by
> Next year, some year
> Though it's hell that I'm going through
> Some Tuesday, Thursday, April, August
> Autumn, winter, next year, some year
> Time heals everything
> Time heals everything
> But loving you."

The key to that song is in the last line. But if you want that line to wipe out your audience, you have to build to it and you have to understand the courage of the woman who sings it. That's what I explained to Bernadette and to Barbara Cook and Georgia Brown and to all the ladies who have sung this song.

Singers invariably begin this song very weepy and sad. When I am directing them I always stop them and say, "No. This is a person who is being brave and who really believes that she has the strength to get over this terrible heartache. It is only when she gets to the last line that she admits she can't stop loving this man. That is the moment that will break the audience's heart. But if you start out feeling sorry for yourself, you won't move them in the same way."

Even today, I will go to a nightclub and see someone sitting on a stool, weeping through "Time Heals Everything." Of course I would never say anything to them, but I can't help thinking that they don't really understand that song.

I WAS SO thrilled for Bernadette when she was nominated for a Tony. She had not actually been our first choice for Mabel. Our first choice was a girl named Marcia Rodd, but she and Gower did not see eye to eye. Kelly Garrett was our second Mabel, but she and Gower didn't hit it off, either. We were well into rehearsal by this time, and people were starting to call the show *Mack and Maybe*.

I was the one who said to Gower, "How about Bernadette Peters? She has the voice, she has the humor, and she is absolutely unique—which is exactly what Mabel should be." Gower thought it was a wonderful idea. When she came to the Belasco Theater where we were rehearsing, we all held our breath. Gower took her off alone, and when he came back he was smiling.

I couldn't have been more delighted. Bernadette is a darling girl and a hard worker. I loved her sound and it was a joy teaching her the songs.

So WHAT DID we do wrong?

One thing that was wrong was the big age difference between our stars. In real life, there was only about a six-year age difference between Mack Sennett and Mabel Normand. Bob Preston was much, much older than Bernadette. Right from the beginning some people noticed that and said to me,

"That's not a good match." But I wouldn't listen. I just ignored them.

Both actors were so persuasive and so perfectly suited to their roles, it never occurred to me that their ages would be a problem. I don't think any of us even thought about it until we actually saw them on stage and in costume. Bob was a very attractive and virile man, but he looked like Bernadette's grandfather.

There was a bigger problem with the production.

Gower did some brilliant visual effects to make the whole show look like old silent movies. He created this fantastic Keystone Kops sequence that was his pride and joy. The Kops came running when a big fire broke out in a hospital. Bells and sirens went off, there were hoses and ladders everywhere and crazed people were running around in every direction. It was a huge, spectacular piece of work and very cleverly done.

The trouble was that Gower spent more time on this one production number than on the rest of the show—and it didn't work. That number took most of our rehearsal time and most of our preview time before Gower finally realized that you can't make living human beings on a stage look like old movie characters. That was a costly miscalculation.

The set wasn't right, either. Robin Wagner worked imaginatively with a very limiting concept of Gower's, which was to set the action in the corner of a huge soundstage. That device seemed terrifically clever at the time, but proved to be much too static. Actually, it became boring. Those permanent angled walls of our set also made it impossible for us to use the flies to bring in new backdrops and changes of scenery. But by the time we realized that, it was too late.

There were also problems with the book. It was a very bold and interesting piece of work, but I never felt there was enough romance in the first act. It took much too long to get the audience interested in the offbeat love story that was the heart of this piece.

These were problems that could have been corrected out of town, the way we worked out the problems on all my earlier shows. But this time, the process didn't work. Instead, what happened out of town was a pure horror story.

WE STARTED BIG—too big. We opened in San Diego and got terrific reviews. Then we played the Music Center in Los Angeles and were even more successful. Bobby Fryer, who was one of my three *Mame* producers and a very bright, knowledgeable, theater-oriented guy, came running over to me after the opening night in Los Angeles. "Jerry," he said, "this is the biggest hit you have ever had!"

I figured that if Bobby Fryer said so, it must be true. Everybody else was excited, too. The show got beautiful notices and did smash business. If that's the way it went in Los Angeles, I could already see us in New York, serving coffee in the streets again for all the people in the ticket line. I honestly thought I had another hit.

Actually, I thought that I had a hit—with reservations. There were still things that were wrong with the show.

To begin with, Mack and Mabel did not make the most lovable hero and heroine for a musical play. Sennett was this tough, black-Irish businessman who was totally wrapped up in making movies. That's all that he cared about in life. Mabel Normand was more vulnerable and more likeable, but essentially passive.

It's okay to have a hero and a heroine with problem personalities, but it would have been nice to have tried to *solve* their problems. Instead, we killed off the heroine. At the end of the play, Mack turned to the audience and said, "And then, in 1936, Mabel Normand died."

Well, that line used to take all the air out of the audience. You could actually hear them deflating. If they had liked the show up to this point, they hated it after we knocked off Mabel. Who wanted to see that adorable little girl die?

The thing is, it wasn't even true! That never happened in real life. After her affair with Mack Sennett, Mabel Normand married another man. She had a whole new life and probably a pleasant marriage for seven years.

I begged Gower and Mike not to end the show with her death but they insisted. Gower was going through what I call his Chekhov period. He was famous for doing all these big, bouncy musicals, and I think he liked *Mack and Mabel* because it was more serious. But he wanted to take it one step further, to make it even darker.

We knew what our problems were—what some of them were, anyway—and now it was time for us to get down to work and fix them. Instead, we went to St. Louis.

THIS WAS A very uncharacteristic move for David Merrick, because regardless of my past problems with him, he is an extremely intelligent man and a very sharp producer. But instead of letting us sit down in one place to do our work, he booked the show into theaters across the country. It probably looked like a smart financial move, but it turned out to be a blunder.

So, here we were at the MUNI Opera in St. Louis, which is this immense outdoor arena and the absolute worst place in the world to work on a new musical. The place was so enormous that it ripped the performances apart. Bob Preston couldn't bring out the subtle qualities of his character, and Bernadette couldn't just be her simple, delightful self. No actor can be simple or subtle on that gigantic stage. They have to throw out their arms and raise their voices to reach 11,000 people. They have to *overact*—and it pulled the show completely out of shape.

When we got to Washington, we tore the show apart again to fix things that didn't even need fixing. When Gower got all excited and said, "Let's get rid of this . . . let's change that," you wanted to do it. You wanted to be a good collaborator and help out.

The songs were working, so I didn't have to fiddle with the score very much. But Gower made me get rid of "Hit 'Em on the Head" and replace it with "Every Time a Cop Falls Down" for the Keystone Kops number. The original number was working beautifully, but Gower was afraid to use this piece of choreography that he thought was too much like a number that Jerome Robbins did years ago in *High Button Shoes*. I kept telling him to do whatever felt natural and right for the material. He went and changed it anyway.

Gower did a charming soft-shoe for the new song, but it never had the vitality of the original Keystone Kops number. That was a loss, not a gain, and it was typical of the tinkering that was done on this show, which was fatally overworked on the road. Instead of concentrating on the true weaknesses, we spent months and months working on unnecessary things.

MACK AND MABEL finally arrived in New York, and for the first and only time in my life, I had a show open on Broadway that was *less* polished and *less* perfect than the production that had gone out of town four months earlier.

On top of everything else, we had an opening night marred by disaster—an onstage accident that was fatal to the show and almost fatal to members of the cast. It happened in the middle of "Tap Your Troubles Away," which is a pivotal number in the middle of Act Two. Lisa Kirk was on stage with all the girls, tapping her heart out, when this huge piece of scenery came crashing down. It was the background set for the number, a massive piece of lumber covered with strips of plastic glitter. The whole thing fell down with a crash.

The accident scared the pants off the cast and everybody else in the Majestic Theater. Lisa stopped tapping, which was only natural because this tremendous thing had crashed right behind her. It had come very close to crushing her and the other girls who were dancing in that number. Everyone on stage was very shaken and the number totally fell apart.

The audience was absolutely stunned. They never recovered and neither did the show.

So it was a flawed production and a flawed opening night. And yet, despite the mistakes and the bad timing and the rotten opening-night luck, there were some things in the show that were absolutely marvelous. Bob Preston was delicious in the Keystone Kops number. Bernadette's "Look What Happened to Mabel" was right on the money. Lisa Kirk was a vivacious Lottie. And the entire "I Won't Send Roses" sequence was absolute perfection. The show almost worked in spite of its problems.

I only wish I could say that everyone recognized and appreciated what we *did* accomplish. Some of the critics did, because we got some gorgeous notices, including a marvelous one from Clive Barnes in the New York *Times*. There were also some carping reviews, but I can't blame them because the show didn't come together. To be honest, *Mack and Mabel* was never as good a show as it was in Los Angeles, and when it got to New York it just didn't find its audience.

WHEN THE TONY Award nominations were announced a few months later, nearly every human being who worked on *Mack and Mabel* received a nomination—the producer, the librettist, the set designer, the costume designer, the director, the choreographer, and the two stars. Everyone except me. To make absolutely sure that I was left out, the nominating committee had to dig up a couple of bombs, *A Letter to Queen Victoria* and *The Lieutenant,* to nominate.

The whole decade of the 1970s was not so hot for me to begin with, but that rejection really hurt me. To tell the truth, it still bothers me.

I was also very angry, because I felt that we had been sold out. There was a booking jam on Broadway and all the big shows were fighting for theaters. We were playing at the Majestic, a Shubert-owned house, and the word around town was that another show wanted to play that house. That wouldn't have mattered if we had been a smash hit. We were getting by and actually building an audience, but the show was what they call a "soft hit," and everybody knew that the Shuberts wanted the theater for *The Wiz.* So we were sacrificed.

That really infuriated me. I mean, here we had this big producer who was *famous* for fighting for his shows. David Merrick was notorious for taking crazy ads and doing all kinds of insane stunts to promote his shows. He put statues of naked women in Central Park for *Fanny.* He ran big quote ads in the newspapers to promote *Subways Are for Sleeping,* using rave reviews from ordinary people who happened to have the same names as the New York critics. But he didn't do a damned thing for *Mack and Mabel.* He didn't even have a three-sheet poster made for the show. The big poster I have hanging on my wall is from the Washington production.

MACK AND MABEL ran for about six months and then disappeared—for a while. But I wasn't the only one who couldn't forget about that show. Right from the beginning there were theater professionals who wanted to work on that piece and do it again. Some people were really passionate about it.

Ron Field, a wonderful choreographer and director who is not with us anymore, did the first "corrective" production, with Luci Arnaz and David Cryer. A few years later, the Papermill Playhouse did another version using some new material. "Hit 'Em on the Head" went back into the show for that one, and Lee Horsley was a marvelous Mack. That was the production that showed me what I needed to do to fix the show. Around that same time Richard Digby Day also did a production in England that had some interesting new ideas.

And then, ten years after *Mack and Mabel* opened and closed on Broadway, the most amazing thing happened. The British ice-skating team of Torvil and Dean skated to the overture from the original cast album when they won the 1984 Olympic gold medal for figure skating. That event was broadcast on BBC Television, and the very next day the BBC was inundated with calls from viewers who wanted to know what the music was and where they could buy it. There was such a major run on the album in record stores that the record company rushed to re-release the album. It sold like crazy in England and made it to number six on the charts, which is unheard of for a show album—especially one that was ten years old.

Suddenly, everybody was *Mack and Mabel* crazy. The show was a true cult hit in London, and people kept besieging me for a production. I would get letters from people in England who were almost indignant that there were no plans to produce the show. "Well, where *is* it?" they would say to me. "Isn't it ready *yet?*"

In 1988, Barry Mishon, Don Pippin, and I finally put together this big charity concert for one night only at the Theatre Royal, Drury Lane. We had dozens of British and American stage performers, a different star for every number.

George Hearn sang "Movies Were Movies." Georgia Brown did "Time Heals Everything." Tommy Tune tap-danced to "Tap Your Troubles Away." The audience was in heaven, and for me it was pure bliss.

The show was a one-night wonder. Sheridan Morley, who is the drama critic of *Punch* and the London theater correspondent for the *International Herald-Tribune*, called the score "one of the richest and most distinctive in the whole postwar history of Broadway" and identified me as "the greatest working Broadway songwriter in the Irving Berlin tradition of sheer orchestral entertainment."

THE ENGLISH WERE so nuts about *Mack and Mabel*, it seemed absolutely right to me that they should be the ones to finally do what may well be the definitive production of that show. I am talking about the 1995 London revival.

It took producers Jon Wilner and Peter LeDonne about eight years to get the production off the ground, but it finally opened at the Piccadilly Theater with Howard McGillin as Mack and this sensational Australian actress, Caroline O'Connor, as Mabel. Francine Pascal, who is Mike Stewart's sister, reworked the book, and I went over to work on the production.

The show now ends when Mabel returns to Mack's studio to make her comeback movie. Mack knows that the project is hopeless and will ruin him financially, but he makes the movie anyway. It's an enormous gesture of love from the man who sang "I Won't Send Roses" to let Mabel know that he would never be able to tell her he loved her. What a powerful emotional moment for the end of a love story!

They did it first in Leicester, a very dull English town about an hour from London that happens to have a terrific theater and an excellent director, Paul Kerryson. I came in at the very

199

beginning of rehearsals because there were new orchestrations and a lot of other technical work for me to do. That just about wore me out, but I wouldn't have missed it for the world. The run was completely sold out before it even opened.

The word had got out from Leicester to London, and the $1.57 million advance at the Piccadilly Theater topped *Crazy for You*, which was the big musical hit in town that season. With all that word building, the London opening night was like a royal event. Half of the New York theater community came over and everybody was dressed to the nines in long gowns and tuxedos. We even had horse-drawn carriages to take everyone to the party.

I don't think I will ever hear that score sung as gorgeously as it was that night. Howard McGillin sang "I Won't Send Roses" thrillingly, and the audience went nuts for Caroline O'Connor, who has a Judy Garlandy sort of voice that is really exciting. She was Mabel right down to her fingernails. It also pleased me to see how everyone got the subtlety of the songs.

When they called me up on the stage for a curtain call, I could feel my face grinning from ear to ear. I was so happy I thought I would burst.

One reviewer said that "on a feel-good scale, it ranks higher than any musical this century." I could bless the critic on the *Financial Times* for what he said about me as a songwriter. "The brio and intelligence of Jerry Herman's lyrics," he wrote, "match the songs with a fizz that has seldom been found in the musical theatre of the last thirty years." A couple of weeks later, the show won the London *Evening Standard* Award for Best Musical.

I THINK IT'S pretty wonderful that *Mack and Mabel* finally found its audience—even if it took twenty-one years. I hate to pick favorites, which is like saying that you love one of your children more than the others, but I have to admit that *Mack and Mabel* is my favorite score. I love that show and I never gave up my belief in it. It was my obsession to bring that show back to life.

Now, I think of it as my fourth big hit. We were able to turn a 1974 failure into a 1995 hit—which is absolutely unheard of in this business—and from now on, that musical will never more be perceived as a failure. This is one of the rare times that such a thing has happened in the American musical theater, and it is probably the single most gratifying accomplishment of my career.

I also feel personally vindicated. After all these years, my hurt and disappointment are finally over.

NOBODY KNOWS THIS, but for several years after *Mack and Mabel* I was too depressed to work. That original failure was the heartbreak of my career, and it made me so miserable that I truly did not want to write anymore. If I could do the finest work of my career and get the brush-off, then maybe I was in the wrong business.

Since my three Broadway hits had made me financially secure and independent, I didn't have to write any more to make a living if I didn't want to. And for a little while, I didn't. Instead, I went to Hollywood.

THIRTEEN

"I Belong Here"

Most people go to Hollywood to make movies. I went to Hollywood to buy houses.

"Home" was now this New York townhouse I owned at 219 East Sixty-first Street, but for about four years I spent a lot of time in California. I would buy a lovely house, transform it into something truly stunning, and then sell it to someone for a lot of money. This wasn't some hobby, you understand. It became my profession. My work was published in about fifteen magazines and I won a prestigious award from Parsons School of Design. I worked full-time at this second career, and I made lots and lots of money at it.

One of my first houses had once belonged to Elizabeth Taylor and Michael Wilding. It had been their honeymoon house. The location was fabulous—way up at the very top of Beverly Hills—but the place itself was run down and no longer a very interesting house. I bought it because it was the finest piece of land in Hollywood. You could wake up in the morning, take your cup of tea outside, and look out at the Pacific Ocean. It had a view of the world.

What a number I did on that house! I redid it from top to bottom and turned it into an English gentleman's country

203

house. I put down beautiful wood floors, covered the walls with gorgeous imported fabric, and furnished the place with many fine old pieces that had been handed down from generation to generation. The decor was quietly elegant. And of course, everything was very comfortable and cheery. If I were designing a palace, it would still have to be cozy.

I loved living in that house. That's the way I work, by the way—I move into a house and I go to work. Sometimes I will do two houses at the same time, but usually I live in one house while I am working on it, and then move on to another project. My Bel Air home, where I live now, is my twenty-sixth.

So there I was, living on top of the world in the Elizabeth Taylor house. After a while, I felt it was time to go on, so I put the house on the market. But it was a very expensive property and in the mid–1970s the California real-estate market was floundering, so I really worried about being able to sell it. I didn't have to worry long, though, because that was the house I sold to Bubbles Rothmere in that taxicab ride to the London opening of *Dolly!*

IN A WAY, doing houses is like doing a Broadway musical, only without the chorus girls. You have to love the property and give it all your time and concentration. And if you want to make the work interesting you have to keep trying something new. You have to make it a challenge for yourself.

When I wrote *Dear World*, I gave myself the assignment of writing an elegant little chamber musical. The challenge of *Hello, Dolly!* was to make it feel like turn-of-the-century New York. For *Mack and Mabel*, the music and lyrics had to be faithful to the era of the silent pictures. It's the same way with the houses. I've done them in many different styles: English country estate, sophisticated New York penthouse, ultra-modern beach house. I've restored historic houses, too, and won prizes for them.

Sometimes I am inspired by the architecture of the house, sometimes by the setting. I remember vividly one little house on Londonderry Place in Los Angeles. Howard Hughes had built it for one of his mistresses. The house was very modern and eccentric, because it was built over a swimming pool. It was not a big house and it didn't come with much land. So no matter which room you were in, or where you thought you were headed, you always ended up in the swimming pool. The pool was the centerpiece of that place—which probably gives you an idea of how Howard Hughes and his mistress spent their time.

One of my most ambitious designs was this 1930s Art Deco penthouse that I did in New York. It was right after *Mack and Mabel* closed and I needed a project. So I bought this penthouse apartment in a stunning Art Deco building at 55 Central Park West. The woman who sold it to me had lived there for most of her lifetime. She had done practically nothing to the place, which had lots of tiny, undistinguished rooms. But the apartment came with a roof garden that I knew I could turn into something marvelous.

I made up my mind that this was going to be a major project, so I called my friend Chuck Fultz, who had worked with me on many other design projects. I moved in and started ripping the place completely apart. I really poured myself into that project. It wasn't musical theater, but it gave me something creative to wake up to every morning. Not only did I design that job, I also contracted it, shopped it, and oversaw all the work. It took twelve workmen working full time and I don't know how many months—but it was spectacular.

When the job was finished, I had knocked down eight tiny rooms into four huge, gorgeous spaces with glorious views of

Central Park. The new rooms had very sleek lines and I did it all in gray flannel, with big Lucite coffee tables. My favorite touch was a Lucite bannister, imbedded with tiny white lights, that led up to a fantastic roof garden where I used to throw fabulous parties. The whole environment was very smart and very dramatic. You kept expecting Fred and Ginger to come floating down the stairs and waltz across the floor. Actually, you were more likely to run into Superman and Lois Lane, because the movie studio used my terrace as a set for that film.

I lived very happily for a while on this spectacular stage set that I had built—and then I sold it to Calvin Klein and moved on.

WHAT I DIDN'T understand back then, and what I am admitting to myself only now, is that a lot of what I was doing was sublimation. I told myself that my talent for design was another side of my creativity and that decorating houses was just as exciting and creative as writing musicals.

The truth is, I was afraid to write.

I turned down every theater project that came along, because I honestly believed that I was just not interested in writing for the theater anymore. Part of the creative psyche, I guess, is that we are sensitive people. My sensitivity turned me off writing. And also the fear of having another failure. That, too.

I realize now that working on all those houses was taking the place of doing what I should have been doing, which was writing musical theater. But my design work was creative, too, and renovating those houses gave me enormous pleasure.

So I really don't regret my houses. In fact, I recently finished a glass-and-stone extravaganza in Palm Springs. It was built by Dinah Shore and it sits on a two-acre parklike piece of property with mature citrus trees, a rose garden, a fifty-foot swimming pool, a tennis court—the works.

* * *

I HAD OTHER projects to keep me busy, too.

The Broadway producer Jimmy Nederlander had put up the money for a major production of *Hello, Dolly!* starring Carol Channing by the Houston Grand Opera Company. Gower Champion had passed away, so Mr. Nederlander asked me to supervise the production. That was a huge challenge for me, being completely in charge of my own show. But I took to it like a baby duck to a puddle of water.

I had never been happy with the orchestration of "Ribbons Down My Back," which I thought was weak and uninteresting, so I was able to make this change and improve several other things, too. I always wanted the show to have an overture, so I added one. It was also lovely working with Florence Lacey. She was the gorgeous actress with the brilliant voice whom I met at Rock Hudson's Christmas party. I cast Florence as Mrs. Molloy, and finally I had a *sexy* Mrs. Molloy! And my pal Lee Roy Reams was perfect as Cornelius.

The critics praised my production, which made me very proud. Some of them even said it was better than the original. In the history of the American musical theater, maybe the 1978 Houston Grand Opera production of *Hello, Dolly!* is no big deal. But it will always mean something special to me because I have never been so totally and intimately involved in a stage production.

BECOMING A PERFORMER was another new experience for me.

The only time I had ever done such a thing was when we were trying to raise the money for *Mack and Mabel*. I had never felt secure singing my own material, because I was not blessed with a great voice, so I would always hire great voices for our backers' auditions. But at one of these auditions the male singer felt under the weather and conked out at the last minute. It was just like that scene from *42nd Street* when Ruby Keeler has to take over for the star who sprains her ankle. David Merrick turned to me and said, "Kid, you've got to go on."

No one knew what a panic I was in when I went on as Mack. No miracle happened to give me a voice like Pavarotti, but I sang the role with the kind of passionate conviction that, even more than a beautiful voice, gave the audience the essence and the intent of the material. It must have worked, because we took in all the rest of the backing we needed at that audition.

That modest debut gave me the courage to say yes when I was asked to perform at Rainbow and Stars in 1989. Rainbow and Stars is this terribly elegant supper club in New York, and it was their idea to have me do a nightclub act of my stuff. To my own surprise, I said I would.

I asked Karen Morrow and Lee Roy Reams to do the show with me, because I think they are the essence of great musical comedy singing. We had ourselves a time! The show got ecstatic notices and was so popular that they held us over for six weeks and we made a recording. And then they made us bring it back, this time with Florence Lacey, for *another* six weeks.

That was marvelous for me, because it was the first time in my life that I had ever performed my material in public. It was a very curious sensation, because I had never been that close to an audience before. I was still squeamish about my singing, until I realized that these people genuinely liked hearing me sing and tell my anecdotes. They especially loved it when I sang "Mame," because it was coming from the person who actually wrote it.

That experience made me realize that I could actually go out there in public and sing and carry on. We did the show again in

Dallas and in Miami and at the New Opera House in San Francisco. Every once in a while I will pick it up again and do it somewhere else. That show has become a staple in my life.

THAT KIND OF intimate involvement with my own work was impossible in Hollywood. In fact, it's exactly the opposite in films. On Broadway, I was in a position to say no to anything I didn't like—anything at all. As the composer-lyricist, I could say no to casting Madonna in one of my shows, if I felt like it.

In Hollywood, it didn't matter one bit what I liked or didn't like. That was the tough lesson I had to learn when Warner Brothers made the movie version of *Mame*.

Once again, I had sold my film rights for a lot of money. Although Warner Brothers hired me as musical supervisor, I had absolutely no say-so on the film. I was hoping they would cast Angela Lansbury as Mame, but no one from the movie studio ever consulted me about anything. One day, they just announced that Lucille Ball had been cast as the star of the movie.

When I heard that, I very bravely took myself to Warner Brothers and made an appointment with one of their top executives. I honestly forget this man's name. All of these Hollywood people come and go out here, and he was just one of those people who came and went.

"It is probably too late to do anything about it," I told this man, "but as one of the authors of this piece, I would like to tell you why I think you have made a big mistake in casting Lucille Ball." Before he could say a word, I told him how much I adored Lucille Ball and what a great clown she was.

"But Mame Dennis is not a clown," I told him. "She is an elegant woman, and when she slides down the bannister it's funny *because* she's an elegant woman. It won't be funny when

Lucille Ball slides down the bannister because she is always doing much more outrageous things than that.

"And besides," I finished up my little speech, "Lucille Ball can't sing and she can't dance. So will you *please* tell me why you have cast her in my show?"

Well, that was the end of our friendly meeting. This person who had been so polite when I walked into his office and introduced myself suddenly became very cold and businesslike.

"We are in the motion picture business," he told me. "We have to think beyond the artistic angle. We have to think about who is going to sell tickets, and I tell you that Lucille Ball is going to sell tickets." And then he dismissed me, the way my English teacher Miss Sirota used to dismiss me after class.

His last words were, "One day you are going to thank me." I never saw the man again.

I CAN'T TELL you what a painful experience it was for me, trying to teach Lucille Ball the score of *Mame*. She tried very hard—I have to say that for her. She sat down with me every day in the studio and she worked her ass off. I liked her for that, and we became very nice friends. But she just couldn't sing it. She didn't have the vocal cords.

To this day, nobody knows what I had to do behind the scenes to get Lucy's voice on that soundtrack.

One day, she was trying to sing the line, "Open a new window, open a new door," but she just couldn't hear that half-tone on *door*. I managed to teach her every other note, but she just couldn't get that half-tone. The poor woman was in agony. So was I.

Finally, I said, "Look, Lucy, I'll tell you what you can do. You can sing 'Open a new window, open a new—' and then stop. Don't sing that last note, and I promise you I will fix it."

She was relieved but baffled. She kept saying, "Are you sure? Are you *sure* that's what you want me to do?"

I got her to sing the line without the final note, and then I sent her home. When she came in the next day, I played a note on the piano and said, "Sing *'door.'*" She didn't have any frame of reference, so she didn't recognize the half-tone. But she did it. She sang, *"Door."*

I said, "Thank you," and clipped the note into the track. I clipped the entire soundtrack together that way.

THE MOVIE OF *Hello, Dolly!* was another heartbreaker, in spite of the fact that it had the great Streisand playing Dolly Levi. That incredible woman belted out song after song and knocked my socks off. She held that last note of "Parade" for sixteen bars. It seemed to go on forever. That was glorious—and it was done in one take! She also turned "So Long, Dearie" into a showstopping tour de force.

But Gene Kelly, who directed, did not want to have anything to do with me. It wasn't that he hated me personally, he just didn't want his movie to be contaminated by anyone from Broadway.

Gene Kelly wasn't the only one who had that old anti-Broadway bias. So many of these movie people are like that. I got the same cold reception on both films of my shows, and I am not the kind of person who generally gets a cold reception, because the smart ones know that I can be very helpful. But these Hollywood types didn't like *any* theater people. They considered us the enemy—and that's the God's truth.

On one of the few occasions when Gene Kelly would even let me speak with him, I tried to tell him something about "Just Leave Everything to Me," which was the opening song that I wrote for Barbra Streisand. I had written it for a specific place, very early in the movie. But instead of using it where it belonged, he put it before the main titles.

I was very polite and did not lose my temper, but I quietly pointed out to Mr. Kelly that if he took that song out of the scene I wrote it for, there would be no music for the first half-hour of the movie. He gave me the cold shoulder, which offended me deeply, because I was giving good advice and I knew it.

Gene Kelly knew it, too. But he wouldn't admit it until we were sitting together at the Hollywood premiere in the Rialto Theater. It was a wonderful opening sequence—beautiful titles, gorgeous photography, and a grand entrance from Barbra—followed by a solid half-hour of talk. I sat there fuming.

He had the gall to turn to me and say, "You know, I should have put the song there." I wanted to hit him.

That's the way it goes in Hollywood. The people can be infuriating and the business can drive you crazy. But you have to laugh, because there is something so endearing about the movies themselves.

I put my own affection for the Hollywood movie in "Just Go to the Movies," a song that I wrote for *A Day in Hollywood,* which was this very smart musical revue with Tommy Tune that Alex Cohen produced on Broadway in 1980. I love to sing it at parties.

"Need to relax? Need to escape?
Go see Fay Wray in the paw of an ape
Watch Errol Flynn shooting his bow
Just go to the movies
Just go to a picture show, oh
When your morale needs some repairs
Watch Busby's beauties descending the stairs
Hundreds of girls doin' high kicks
Just go to the movies
Just go to the flicks.

> Girls in sarongs
> Monsters in capes
> See Scarlett make a dress out of the drapes. . . ."

The lyrics go on and on, and friends of mine have their favorite lines that they keep quoting at me. Somebody recently sent me a little notecard with a picture of these glittery red shoes on the front. Inside, this person had written:

> Whenever you're down in the dumps
> Try putting on Judy's red pumps.

BUT IT'S NO wonder that people from New York get so frustrated when they come out here. Hollywood movie people don't work the same way that we do in the theater.

In my experience, the basic difference between working with creative collaborators on a Broadway show and working in Hollywood on film and television projects is the corporate interference. Your work becomes much more difficult because you have to please so many executives who need to make every little show into a big corporate enterprise. Instead of having to satisfy one or two tough producers, the way it is on Broadway, you have to worry about keeping all these executives happy. That is just the way it works, but it is very complicated—and terribly frustrating.

One project I have been happy working on is the television Christmas special called *Mrs. Santa Claus* that I wrote for Angela Lansbury. That was my first television project, and I was so pleased that the package was put together by my agent Priscilla Morgan—the same William Morris agent who discovered me all those years ago at my first off-Broadway show, *I Feel Wonderful*. To this day, Priscilla remains my loyal supporter and number-one fan.

My collaborators, Mark Saltzman and Robert L. Freedman, and I worked on *Mrs. Santa Claus* exactly the way that collaborators work on musical theater pieces—we sat down in a deli and racked our brains for an idea. Mark was the one who came up with the notion of doing a piece about Mrs. Santa Claus. Then I jumped in with my ideas about this character.

"Can't you just imagine how frustrated she must be?" I said. I could almost see her, stuck in that kitchen up in the North Pole for who knows how many centuries, baking cookies and wrapping Christmas presents. Nobody knows about this poor lady, or even thinks about her. All they're thinking about is her husband, Mr. Claus, who neglects her because his job keeps him so busy. "This woman needs to get out of the house," I said to Mark.

We had great fun tossing around ideas, which is what they call a "story conference" out here.

I had an unusually positive experience with the CBS executives on *Mrs. Santa Claus,* and I started to get used to these corporate meetings. After Mark and I came up with our idea, all these important people came over to my house so we could tell them our story and I could play them the seven songs I had written. Once more, my friend Alice Borden was sitting by my side at the piano. When they all filed into my projection room, it was like a convention.

The network bigwigs were all here. The head of the CBS entertainment division came with his various assistants. The president of the William Morris Agency was also here, along with all *his* assistants. And then there were the people from Angela's company, Corymore Productions. They were here, too.

We were fortunate with *Mrs. Santa Claus* because once they heard our material, all these executives went bananas over the show. They have been very supportive of the project right from the start. Angela loves the show and we're having a grand time getting it ready for Christmas, 1996.

I HAVE TO say one thing about Hollywood—coming out here in the 1970s was wonderful for my social life. I met a lot of nice people and had some lovely romances. Like everyone else in those days, I was very free sexually. If you were gay, the '70s were a terrific time to party.

People were constantly calling me to go out and I found that I was very much in demand in Hollywood celebrity circles. I also had a wonderful group of close friends in San Francisco, so I would go up there on weekends and enjoy all *that* craziness. I mean, I was having fun. I was a happy man.

Of course, I was not afraid of things I should have been more careful about—but no one else was, either, because nobody knew then about AIDS or the HIV virus.

AT THE SAME time that I was playing with my houses and enjoying my terrific social life, I was also depressed about my work.

The year after *Mack and Mabel* failed on Broadway, *A Chorus Line* opened in 1975 and people went crazy. They said it was a new era in the American musical theater. Suddenly, everybody started doing no-book musicals like *Ain't Misbehavin'* and all-dance shows like Bob Fosse's *Dancin.'* I didn't see a place for me in this new era.

The music that people admired were operatic scores like Stephen Sondheim's *Sweeney Todd* and Andrew Lloyd Webber's *Evita*. Everybody was fascinated by this new sound, this new style of work. I was out of fashion because that was not my sound or my style. I was still back there with Irving Berlin.

Don't get me wrong—that was exactly where I *wanted* to

be. I would be happy if I could write something like "I'll be loving you always" for the rest of my life. That's what I want my ballads to sound like, because that's what I think the American showtune is all about—and because that's what I personally love.

I couldn't change my style or my taste even if I wanted to, and that's why I felt so totally out of it. I felt that it had all happened too late for me. If I had only started out in the 1930s, or even the 1940s, I might have written twenty shows, because that was my true musical era. That's when they were writing the songs I loved and the kind of entertainment that I wanted to keep alive.

In a way, I did accomplish my goal, because my shows helped to keep that style of music alive through the 1960s, the 1970s, and as late as the 1980s. With all this new enthusiasm in the 1990s for *Hello, Dolly!* and *Mack and Mabel*, maybe that style will even survive into the next century.

But when you feel that you are one of the only ones left writing that kind of music, it can be very lonely.

I WAS TIRED of my professional exile in Hollywood, and at that point in my life I made a dreadful mistake. I wrote a show for the wrong reasons. I did not agree to do this show because I loved the material but because I loved the people I would be working with.

The show was *The Grand Tour*.

My collaborator Michael Stewart called me up one day and said, "Jerry, I have a show for you. It's based on the S. N. Behrman play called *Jacobowsky and the Colonel*."

"That's a lovely play and it will probably make a very interesting musical," I told him, "but I really don't want to write a musical about some man who is running from the Nazis. I would rather do something with showgirls."

He said, "Okay, forget about it," and I forgot about it.

Weeks went by. I was busy doing my houses, enjoying my hectic social life, and running around the country overseeing all these productions of *Dolly!* and *Mame*. So I really did not give it a thought. Then I got another call from Mike.

"We've got the money," he said. "We've got the Palace Theater. We've got Joel Grey."

"I like everything you're telling me," I said to him, "but you know, this is still a show about a guy who is running from the Nazis."

So, over he came with Diana Shumlin, this lovely lady who was the producer of the show, and the two of them proceeded to charm the pants off me. At one point, Mike turned to me and said, "Come on, Jerry! It's going to be you and me again. We'll have a good time. It'll be fun!"

I said, "Well, let me read it again." And the next day I said yes.

I feel badly saying that I like *The Grand Tour* less than my other shows, because that show is one of my children, too, and there are some lovely things in it. The story, which is about the relationship of this aristocratic Polish colonel and this little Jewish refugee, is actually quite charming. It has humor and a lot of heart.

But I have to say that I never had a passion for the piece, and I think it shows. When you have true love for something and go at it with passion, it always shows in the work.

AT LEAST *The Grand Tour* got me writing again. I don't mean to say that I went all those years, between *Mack and Mabel* in 1974 and *The Grand Tour* in 1979, without having music in my life. I am almost physically attached to the piano and I sit and play for hours every single day. Sometimes I play my own stuff and sometimes I play Kander and Ebb, Bock and

Harnick, Strouse and Adams, Burton Lane, and all the other songwriters I admire. I love to play showtunes, and sometimes I just play to play. That's how I get a lot of emotion out. Even when I stopped writing for the theater, I never turned off the music in my life.

Writing music is a different thing, though, because I don't write "songs." I never sit down at the piano and say, "I am going to write a song today." The way I think, musically, is always in terms of theater pieces and theatrical characters.

So I have to say that it was nice to be back at work on a theater piece after five years. The songs for *The Grand Tour* came very naturally. I adore "I Belong Here" and I think I did good work on pieces like "I'll Be Here Tomorrow" and "Marianne" and "You I Like." It was also very pleasant to be working with Mike Stewart and his friend Mark Bramble.

Compared to the *sturm und drang* on some of my shows, the out-of-town tryout for *The Grand Tour* was uneventful. Gerald Freedman did an intelligent job of directing, and he didn't lose his mind on the road like some of them. For me, it was even more enjoyable because I had friends in the cast. My best friend Carol Dorian was in the chorus and my love, Florence Lacey, was playing the female lead opposite Joel Grey. I remember staying at this elegant little hotel in San Francisco and quite enjoying myself.

We had work to do, of course, because the notices in San Francisco were not great. Not bad, but not great. We all agreed that we needed a comedy song, so I wrote a hotel-room song called "Mrs. S. L. Jacobowsky" for Joel Grey to sing when the Jewish refugee he plays decides that he wants to marry a Christian wife.

> "See that lovely lady in the living room
> Lighting up the evening with her youthful bloom
> From her graceful manner you may well presume

That's Missus S.L. Jacobowsky.
We'll artfully combine
Her old world with mine
We'll hang a crucifix in one room
A mezuzah in the sun room
If Reba Jacobowsky could look down and see
This miracle of miracles that's come to me
She'll gladly have a *shiksa* in the family
A girl who'll bring such magic to my life
I'll go to Mass and I'll respect her wishes
And she'll start using sep'rate dishes
When Missus Jacobowsky is my wife.
And when it's almost over and I'm gray and bent
Trying to remember where the years all went
Trying to recall how much each moment meant
And looking for the meaning of my life
When not a soul remembers what my name is
My one lasting claim to fame is
Missus Jacobowsky was my wife."

The work we did on the road was very positive, and *The Grand Tour* was a stronger and a better show when it came into New York in 1979. It got nice notices because it was a nice show. Nice material, nice performances, nice production. It just didn't have the energy and the excitement to become a real hit. It lacked that spark that makes a show explode.

And it turned out that I was right all along about the story, which is basically about this man who is running away from danger. We all did what we could do. I even wrote a carnival number to break the monotony. But the action was just too static and the scenes too repetitive.

The Grand Tour was a mistake. I'm glad that I wrote some of those songs, but I should never have agreed to do that show in the first place. And now here I was, with my third failure in a row.

* * *

I WASN'T DEVASTATED, the way I was after *Mack and Mabel.*
Dolly! and *Mame* were being performed all over the place, and
the song royalties were pouring in from all my shows. But I
still had this feeling that people didn't want my style of writing
anymore. Maybe there was no place in the musical theater for
the kind of stuff I liked to write. Maybe there was no place for
me. I was afraid that maybe it was all over for me.

But I'm the kind of person who picks himself up when he's
down. I always allow myself to be unhappy, but I never let
anything get me down completely. Something in me always
wakes up and says, "Okay, Jerry, get up. You can't sit there
and say your life is over. That's stupid. There are too many
good things ahead."

How could I complain after all my fabulous success? I had
been elected into the Theater Hall of Fame and the Songwriters Hall of Fame, and I had written two shows that had run
over 1,500 performances. It was sad if no one wanted my work
anymore, but with all these goodies that I had acquired during
such a glorious career, I really couldn't agonize over the end of
it.

But when I said yes to *The Grand Tour,* I discovered that
there was still some little spark in me that wanted to go ahead
and write anyway. Maybe the cycle would turn, or maybe there
were still some theatergoers who would welcome a new traditional score. And maybe I just needed to write, because that's
what I do and what I needed to do.

I didn't realize it at the time, but when I wrote the theme
song for S. L. Jacobowsky, I was actually talking about myself.

> "I'll be here tomorrow
> Alive and well and thriving
> I'll be here tomorrow

It's simply called surviving
If before the dawn
This fragile world might crack
Someone's got to try to put the pieces back
So from beneath the rubble
You'll hear a little voice say
'Life is worth the trouble
Have you a better choice?'
So let the sceptics say
Tonight we're dead and gone
I'll be here tomorrow
Simply going on."

FOURTEEN

"The Best of Times"

"It's rather gaudy but it's also rather grand
And while the waiter pads your check he'll kiss your hand
The clever gigolos romance the wealthy matrons
At La Cage aux Folles
It's slightly Forties and a little bit New Wave
You may be dancing with a girl who needs a shave
Where both the riff-raff and the royalty are patrons
At La Cage aux Folles. . . .
Eccentric couples always punctuate the scene
A pair of eunuchs and a nun with a Marine . . .
It's bad and beautiful, it's bawdy and bizarre
I knew a duchess who got pregnant at the bar
Just who is who and what is what is quite the question
At La Cage aux Folles."

Along with *Mame*, working on *La Cage aux Folles* was the most joyous time of my life. For me, it was the very best of times.

La Cage saved my sanity and put me back on top. I mean, *really* on top. To write a show that runs for five years on Broadway and becomes an international phenomenon—that's the top. To win a Tony Award over five of the most talented composer-lyricists in the business—that's the top. Best of all, this show was an entertainment that also made an important statement about our lives. That was the crowning glory.

I like to think that it was fated for me to write *La Cage*. From the moment I saw the original French film, I had this intense longing to write a musical about those two lovable men and their wonderful story. Sheila Mack was with me when I went to see the film one afternoon in Los Angeles. I remember walking out of the dark movie theater and into the bright California sunlight, and then turning to Sheila and saying: "This is going to be my next musical."

My biggest problem in writing musicals has always been finding the right source material. After looking for nine years for something to write about, I had finally found the perfect subject matter. I knew right away that this material sang.

Everything about this piece felt so fresh. The setting is exotic, the characters are adorable, and the story is funny and touching. It takes place in St. Tropez, where an older homosexual couple, Georges and Albin, own a fashionable nightclub, and it's all about what happens to their relationship when Georges' son decides to marry into this very straight, politically conservative family.

We had never seen characters like this on a Broadway stage. Or a setting like La Cage aux Folles, the nightclub where Albin does his drag act. Besides being glamorous, the drag-club setting also offered me a brand-new milieu to work in. In my mind, I saw all these possibilities for writing something truly original—and very theatrical.

When I got home from the movie theater, I ran to the telephone and called my agent, Lee Stevens, to find out about the rights to the material. I didn't even know who had written the screenplay, but I was crazy to get it.

Twenty-four hours later, Lee gave me a full report—I was too late. The producer Alan Carr had acquired the rights and other people were already working on it. Maury Yeston was the composer and Jay Presson Allen was writing the book. Tommy Tune was supposed to direct. These were all experienced and talented theater people, so I knew it was hopeless.

I was so disappointed, I didn't know how I would ever recover. After searching for nine years, I had finally found maybe the best material of my lifetime—only to be told that I couldn't have it. For the next six months, I turned down everything that came my way. Scripts would land on my desk every day, but I could never read more than six pages of a play before tossing it aside. "It's not *La Cage,*" I would say.

The stuff I was turning down wasn't chopped liver, either. But I am a very single-minded person; if I have something in my heart, I can't even see anything else. And I had this *passion* for *La Cage.* It was love, but it felt like agony because I couldn't have what I loved. Only a few close friends knew what I was feeling.

One night when I was back in New York, I got a phone call from two producer friends, Fritz Holt and Barry Brown. They asked me to dinner at Ted Hook's Backstage, a supper club in the theater district that was popular with everybody in the business. I love going out in New York, and I especially loved going to this place, which is no longer around, because I would always run into about a hundred people I knew. So we made the date.

When I got to the club and sat down at the table with Fritz and Barry, they asked me their question right off the bat: "Jerry, do you have any interest in writing the score for *La Cage aux Folles?*"

I thought I would go through the floor.

ONCE THE WORD was out that I was working on this material, people kept telling me that I was doing something ground-breaking. I was writing the first Broadway musical about two men who love each other.

La Cage is a gay love story. But it is much more than that. The hero of that show is a gay man who finds his pride by challenging his own son's bigotry toward homosexuals. The moral of the piece is actually very wholesome, because it is about standing up for yourself and fighting bigotry. In the beginning, people were shocked when they heard about the gay romance and the homosexual themes. But once they became involved in these people's lives, they realized that the human issues applied to everybody—not just homosexuals.

I think everybody working on the project was aware, on some level, of the importance of what we were doing—the chorus kids, our two stars George Hearn and Gene Barry, our director Arthur Laurents, Harvey Fierstein, who wrote the book, and me too. But we were not gung-ho about delivering a political message. We were not out to change the world and wipe out bigotry overnight. We were just doing a musical.

There was a strong feeling of camaraderie on this show. We may have been three gay men, but you couldn't have found three more diverse individuals to put together on a project.

What an unlikely trio we were! Arthur Laurents is from the Leonard Bernstein/Stephen Sondheim school of musical theater. Coming from that literate world of traditional theater, Arthur represents the best of that classy Old Guard generation. Harvey Fierstein was the flashy young comet who burst on the theater scene with *Torch Song Trilogy,* a gay man who is more in touch with the modern theatrical trends and the political views of the younger generation. As a person, Harvey is full of humor and pizzazz, and about as different from the elegant Mr. Laurents as you can get.

And in the middle you have me, Mr. Show Business, the razzmatazz musical-comedy writer, a cheerful man whose life is dedicated to making people smile and feel good and leave the theater humming a showtune.

The three of us didn't have a thing in common—except the passion we had for this show.

OUR COLLABORATION WORKED because we all respected each other, learned from each other, and shared our ideas with each other. We pulled this off because we agreed to put aside any individual political agendas and make *La Cage* appealing to the broadest mass audience.

The material was so rich, we could have done it lots of different ways. We could have toned down the humor, given it a much more serious tone, or made it more romantic, or more politically militant. The material seemed to us to work best as a charming, colorful, great-looking musical comedy—an old-fashioned piece of entertainment.

That suited me, because I like to say things quietly, almost subliminally. I feel that's the way to really get into a person's heart. In the case of *La Cage*, I wanted to write a show about two sweet men that the audience would love and take into their hearts. That's the real secret of getting your point across—not by hitting people over the head with some pedantic lesson, but by making them fall in love with your characters.

I personally never agonized about whether *La Cage* would alter people's attitudes and lifestyles. It was only later, from the audience reaction, that I realized we had written something that could actually change some people's prejudices about homosexuality.

In my own case, I consider myself blessed because I chose a career field where I have always been accepted for what I am, which is a member of two minority groups. You almost *had* to be Jewish to be a Broadway songwriter. So I never had to overcome any professional prejudice on that count.

As for being gay, nothing could be more natural in the world where I live and work. So I never had any traumas about that, either. Being gay was something that went along with me, like my brown hair and the shape of my jaw. In the theater, where you can't find a Broadway show without gay people, nobody thought it was the least bit peculiar.

Just the same, I am conscious that there are always people who would attack and persecute gays, just as there are always people who would attack and persecute Jews. In my own experience, I learned about prejudice at an early age, when a group of neighborhood boys threw stones at me on my way to Hebrew school. But I did not write *La Cage* to make that political point.

If we *had* written a stronger, tougher political message into the material, the New York *Times* might have loved us more. But that would have given our show too narrow an appeal and it would never have found the huge universal audience that it did.

That has always been my answer to those Act Up! gays and other militants who criticized the show because it wasn't "strong enough" and didn't go "far enough." The reason that *La Cage* has been embraced by people all over the world is precisely because it *doesn't* preach. That show has done more good for gays and for the whole gay cause because it shows people that someone's sexuality doesn't determine what makes them a good or a bad person.

That's why that show works in South Africa and Mexico and Brazil and Germany and other countries where you'd think people would be hostile to it. You could have knocked me over when they even played "The Best of Times" at the Republican National Convention. When I watched George and Barbara Bush come out, waving and smiling, I was appalled. But then I thought, "Well, that's the answer to the whole thing, isn't it?

It really is one world after all, and like it or not, we're all joined at the hip because we're human."

You can't find a more universal human feeling than the love and respect for a parent that Georges tries to teach his son in "Look Over There."

"How often is someone concerned with the tiniest thread of your life?
Concerned with whatever you feel and whatever you touch
Look over there
Look over there
Somebody cares that much.
When your world spins too fast
And your bubble has burst
Someone puts himself last
So that you can come first
So count all the loves who will love you from now 'til the end of your life
And when you have added the loves who have loved you before
Look over there
Look over there
Somebody loves you more."

The success of *La Cage* proves that that kind of material is timeless and without boundary. That's why I am so proud of that show—and why I thumb my nose at the people who thought we didn't do enough.

My own concerns about *La Cage* were entirely different, and had to do with the state of the theater in 1983.

I was committed to do the show in the traditional structure of a big, old-fashioned Broadway musical—but I honestly wasn't sure if that could be done anymore. I wondered whether there was still room in the Broadway theater, which

229

had suddenly become so avant garde, for an old-fashioned piece of musical entertainment.

The Broadway musical was going through a new set of changes in the 1980s. We had gotten into the operatic musical, like *Evita,* and the cerebral musical, like *Sunday in the Park with George.* These new developments were healthy and exciting, and I'm not knocking that kind of musical. But it was very different from the sort of thing I write, and I worried about how my work would fit into this new musical scheme. I was concerned that it just might be too late for the world to accept an old-fashioned musical with showtunes like *La Cage.*

I wondered if there was even an audience left for my kind of musical. The Broadway theater started to lose its audience in the 1980s. Audiences were smaller and more fragmented, and I was afraid that the mass audience I write for might have drifted away from Broadway. And what about the audience that was still faithful to the theater—was this material too narrow and too special for them?

The only audience I knew I could count on was the gay audience, which has always been terrifically loyal to musical theater, especially to the entertainments that I write. But I didn't want to patronize the gay audience. I didn't expect them to turn out for *La Cage* just because of its homosexual themes. I wanted them to love the show because it was also a gorgeous entertainment.

ONCE WE KNEW we were a team, Arthur and Harvey and I went right to work in my music studio, upstairs in my brownstone on East Sixty-first Street. We took on the toughest problem first—how on earth were we going to make Albin's transformation from this dowdy, unhappy man in a bathrobe into this glamorous creature called Zsa Zsa?

The first song I wrote for the piece was "A Little More Mascara," a song that got Arthur terrifically excited.

"I want to stage it right in front of the audience," he said. "I want the audience to see every step of Albin's transformation so they'll understand exactly what dressing in drag means to this man."

Well, I was thrilled when I heard that from Arthur, because that idea is about as theatrical as you can get! I knew instantly that I was working with a man after my own heart. Even now, all these years later, I get goosebumps when I think of the brilliant effects that Arthur devised for Albin's transformation number.

As a stager, Arthur was chock full of interesting ideas and he was really cooking on *La Cage*. It was his idea to bring onstage this giant wardrobe full of stunning gowns and shoes and wigs—and to hide people inside the wardrobe to dress Albin. You couldn't even see the hands that came out to zip and tuck him into his clothes. Everything was perfectly synchronized. The stockings had to go on at a very precise moment, and the gloves. The wig was plopped on during a very big note. That was the most spectacular visual effect of all, and it was typical of Arthur, who thinks in visual terms.

Every single word of "A Little More Mascara" was choreographed, musically and visually. It absolutely panicked George Hearn, who said it was the most difficult number he ever had to learn. He had to time every single movement, every dab of lipstick, every touch of eye shadow to a specific lyric. But at the very end of that song—when Albin steps out in all his glory to the line: "And Zsa Zsa is *here!*"—well, you never heard such screaming in your life from an audience.

"A LITTLE MORE MASCARA" was heaven to write, and a special satisfaction for me because in only three minutes of stage time it presents Albin as a three-dimensional character. When the audience watches this unhappy, unattractive man transform himself into this fascinating creature called Zsa Zsa, they understand Albin completely.

> "With a rare combination of girlish excitement
>   and manly restraint
> I position my precious assortment of powders and
>   pencils and paint
> So whenever I feel that my place in the world is
>   beginning to crash
> I apply one great stroke of mascara to my rather
>   limp upper lash
> And I can cope again
> Good God, there's hope again!
> When life is a real bitch again
> And my old sense of humor has up and gone
> It's time for the big switch again
> I put a little more mascara on. . . ."

When Albin sings these thoughts, you realize that this song is not about a man who is putting on a dress. It's about a man who is becoming another human being. During that one sequence, he leaves behind his dull, ordinary middle-aged life and transforms himself into this divine creature who is everything that he thinks of as exquisite and elegant.

To me, that song works because it establishes motive for Albin's transformation. It explains something that the original movie of *La Cage* had treated as a cute, quirky aberration and never did explain—which is *why* a man would want to spend his life in drag.

I certainly don't want to spend *my* life in drag. I am a homosexual man who has never made any bones about his sexuality, but I would be mortified if somebody put a dress on me. I would run for the hills and you wouldn't see me for a month.

There is nothing in me that wants to be a woman. I love being a man who loves women. I like masculine clothes and masculine homes and masculine furnishings.

Albin's needs are different. He *needs* to step into these luxurious gowns and become this ravishing creature we know as Zsa Zsa. That's how he hides his unhappiness and his insecurity, by stepping out of his own skin and becoming another person.

Since clothes were so important to Albin, clothes also became important to us.

We all sat down right at the beginning with Theoni Aldredge, our costume designer, and we agreed that Zsa Zsa's wardrobe had to be very, very glamorous. Theoni was absolutely not going to go for tacky drag, like they always do in films like *Priscilla, Queen of the Desert*. Albin and Georges were wealthy, successful men who had very refined tastes. If Albin had taste, then Zsa Zsa had to have taste, too.

Theoni had some fun designing outrageous numbers for the chorus kids to wear—but the clothes she made for Zsa Zsa were truly *gorgeous*.

I NEVER STRUGGLED for a minute over *La Cage*. The material gave me a lot to say musically, so the songs came very easily—especially with the generous help of my collaborators.

Oscar Hammerstein once said that the most important single word in the language of musical theater is *collaboration*. I read that as a young man and it stayed in my brain. That's the word I think of when I think of *La Cage*, because there was a generosity in the way we worked.

Here's how it happened on one special song: Harvey came in one day with the closing scene of Act One. That's the big dramatic scene when Albin learns that he has not been invited to the wedding of this boy he has raised as his own son. He is terribly embarrassed and hurt. The poor man is completely crushed. But in the middle of this painful moment he has to get out on the stage of this nightclub and entertain the customers.

Harvey read us his scene, and I was struck by one line of dialogue in particular. When he finished, I said to him, "Harvey, I have got to have those five words—'I am what I am'—that you wrote for Albin to say. I want to musicalize that line to close the first act. If you will let me have those five words, I promise you that I will give you a song tomorrow morning."

Well, their eyebrows went up. Harvey said, "Go on—you must be kidding! You are going to write a whole song overnight?" I said, "I can do it, because I am so turned on by the passion of that man's statement and by the powerful situation behind it."

In my view, it is always the situation behind a song—the underpinning, I call it—that makes a song work. If the underpinning is really powerful you could write a lousy song and it might still work.

The setup for "I Am What I Am" is powerful. Here is Albin, this kind, gentle man, who absolutely adores his son—and he finds out that the boy is so ashamed of him for being a drag performer that he does not even want him at his wedding. What an electric moment that is for a song!

My method of writing that particular song was simple. I just went to the piano and poured my heart out. I wrote the whole thing straight through, from the very slow beginning to the big, showtune ending, and I did it overnight—the three choruses, the key changes, even the arrangement. I was hysterical to get it all out of me.

The way we worked, Arthur and Harvey used to come to my house at 11:00 A.M. and we would start talking over an early lunch. But when they arrived on my doorstep the next morning, I said, "We can have lunch later. There's something I want you to hear first." I went to the staircase and they followed me up the four flights to my music studio. I sat them down and took a deep breath.

> "I am what I am
> I am my own special creation
> So come take a look
> Give me the hook or the ovation
> It's my world
> That I want to have a little pride in
> My world
> And it's not a place I have to hide in
> Life's not worth a damn
> 'Til you can say
> 'Hey, world, I am what I am'
> I am what I am
> I don't want praise, I don't want pity
> I bang my own drum
> Some think it's noise
> I think it's pretty
> And so what
> If I love each feather and each spangle
> Why not
> Try and see things from a diff'rent angle
> Your life is a sham
> 'Til you can shout—out loud
> 'I am what I am!' . . ."

Well, that was one of those Big Moments that you live a lifetime for. They screamed, they cried, they carried on like you couldn't believe. It was such a *feeling!*

Then Arthur jumped up and said, "Here's how I see it—on that last big, defiant note, Albin is going to rip off his wig and march right up the aisle of the theater and out the door onto Broadway!" That was such a theatrical image, it blew us away. We carried on like crazy people, insanely happy, crazy people.

That's the kind of thing I'm talking about when I use Oscar Hammerstein's word *collaboration*.

That song started with Harvey's five words. They became my words for a while, because I can identify with Albin too. I have dared to be what I am and to do what I do. It is terribly unfashionable in 1996 to keep writing the way I write. But I have been stubborn enough to go on creating my kind of songs—and to do it my way—regardless of all the fashions and trends.

Then Arthur took up those words and he used them proudly and defiantly by making Albin tear off his wig and march out the theater. "I Am What I Am" is still Albin's song. But now those words belong to every gay man in the world. And beyond that, those words belong to all of us—because that song is every human being's expression of individuality.

PEOPLE HAVE THIS idea about what it's like working on a big Broadway musical. They think there's a lot of high drama during the rehearsals and the tryout period—yelling, screaming, tantrums, and so forth. I had enough of that, thank you, on *Hello, Dolly!* It was nothing like that on *La Cage aux Folles*, which went as smooth as silk.

Arthur Laurents deserves a lot of the credit. Arthur was my choice for director, because I admired him so. Everyone warned me that he was a tough taskmaster, extremely demanding and difficult to work with. Well, he was absolutely devoted to this show. We all were, and that's what made it such an extraordinary experience. We were three gay men writing about something that was very close to us. Nobody's ego was going to get in the way of that camaraderie. No one was going to spoil that.

Another reason that rehearsals went so smoothly had to do

with our stars. It's very interesting how the star of a show can determine the whole temperament of your production. The personality of the star emanates through the company, down to the last member of the chorus. If your star is likeable, there's usually a nice rapport among the whole company. If your star is a brat or a bitch, things can get pretty nasty backstage.

George Hearn and Gene Barry were such sweet, decent people, they set a really nice tone. This was not one of those productions in which the stars acted like stars and kept to themselves. George and Gene were always going out to lunch with us and hanging out with the crew. Everybody liked those two men.

It was Arthur's idea to hire George Hearn for the role of Albin. It was also his idea to get George to do his audition in drag. "Let's do something daring," Arthur said to me. "Let's get our wig and makeup people to work on him for an hour, and then let's get him into costume. You can teach him a song, and I'll give him some basic direction."

Well, here is this very straight, very masculine actor prancing around that rehearsal hall in high heels. He wasn't the least bit shy or embarrassed about being in drag because he accepted it as a challenge, and he delivered "I Am What I Am" with a passion that took our breath away. He had the part in two minutes flat.

George Hearn is a prince, a very liberal thinker who was so unself-conscious about going in drag that he wore a gown to court his wife, Leslie. Leslie was this beautiful girl in the chorus, and everybody in the show knew that George was madly in love with her. We were all whispering about them, because they were so adorable, Leslie with her gorgeous long legs and George in his high heels and beaded gowns. Everybody was so tickled when they got married.

*   *   *

THE REHEARSALS FOR *La Cage* were a dream. Privately, though, I felt that I had to prove something with this show—not to the people out there, but to myself. I had to prove to myself that I could do it again. It wasn't enough to write a show that would get me respectable notices for my score. That wasn't good enough. I wanted to make one last effort to write a theater piece that totally *worked*. I longed to pull that off just one more time.

Maybe that's why I was so insistent about taking *La Cage* out of town.

Going out of town was not a fashionable thing to do in 1983, and of course, it's practically unheard of today. I watch people today struggling to work on their shows in front of the whole city, and it's a nightmare—the theater-party audiences, the people in the business dropping by, the whispers, the gossip, the press. The minute your show opens for previews in New York, people start talking.

That's no atmosphere to work in. It is a very bad system, very damaging to the work.

People don't realize how important that preview period is when you're putting a musical together. It is a crucial time, because that's when you find out what you've actually got. You may think that you have achieved perfection when you look at your show in a rehearsal hall. But you absolutely need to see your work in front of people, because only the audience will tell you the truth. And then you need the time and the distance to do your work in peace.

For that kind of work, you find the best audiences outside New York, in smaller, cosmopolitan cities with a lot of theater lovers. At one time, Philadelphia used to be a nice tryout town. Washington is still good and Boston is wonderful; both these cities have sophisticated audiences and intelligent critics.

Producers always argue economics to get you to stay in Manhattan. But no matter what they try to tell you, the atmosphere is much healthier out of town.

FORTUNATELY FOR ME, the producers of *La Cage* understood the way we needed to work, and they let us take the show to Boston—where I had an experience that I will cherish for the rest of my life.

It was the first preview performance, and I was sitting in the theater waiting for the house to fill up. Arthur Laurents and Harvey Fierstein and I were all huddled together in Row S of the orchestra, clutching each other. It wasn't until this moment when it suddenly hit me that I was in *Boston*—a blue-blooded, conservative, and in some ways prejudiced city—opening a show about *two gay guys*.

I panicked.

"You know, we are crazy, we are truly out of our minds," I started babbling to Arthur and Harvey. "What in the world are we doing in the city of *Boston* with this big musical extravaganza about *transvestites*? Why aren't we, for heaven's sake, in San Francisco?"

The two of them tried to hush me up, but I was in a state. "You know what we are doing here?" I said to them. "We are committing suicide, that's what we are doing here. When those two *men* sit down at that little café table at the edge of the stage and start singing a *love song*, this audience is going to throw stones! And then they are going to get up and walk right out of the theater."

Well, the show started with some nice laughs. The audience loved the opening number with all those fabulous costumes, and they screamed when the wigs came off. For the first fifteen minutes, we were safe.

Then the nightclub scene went off and this pretty scene on

the beach came on. David Mitchell had designed us a charming café with little tables and chairs and strings of colored bulbs and, in the background, the twinkling lights of St. Tropez. The two men were sitting at one of these café tables when Gene Barry, who was playing Georges, began to sing the first bars of "Song on the Sand"—a love song to his male lover. I tell you, my heart was in my mouth.

That's when I spotted them, this couple sitting right in front of us, in Row R. They were the most typical Back Bay Bostonians you could imagine: about sixty years old, the lady with a blue rinse in her hair, the gentleman very distinguished in a blue blazer and his old school tie.

They were *exactly* the kind of people I was worried about. I poked Arthur, and sure enough, he and Harvey had spotted this couple, too. The three of us couldn't tear our eyes away from them.

For the first two minutes of the love song, these two people sat stone-faced. I was *dying*. Then Gene got to the line: "And I'm young and in love"—which he is singing about another *man,* you understand. All of a sudden, this very proper older gentleman took his wife's hand, squeezed it, and gave her a smile.

Harvey and Arthur and I looked at each other, and then the three of us started to bawl. It was *that* kind of moment— maybe the greatest in a lifetime of great show moments. In that instant, I knew in my heart that this show would be accepted anywhere in the world. And we had done it not by being tough and militant, but by being gentle and loving.

"SONG ON THE SAND" is a very important song to me because it says something about my approach to writing. That song is not a gay love song. It is a love song. I wrote that song for any two people who share a memory of being young and walking together on the beach and feeling romantic. It is about that universal human feeling of remembering some magical moment you once shared with someone you love.

First and foremost, I wrote that song for Albin and Georges. I needed to find something for those two characters that would express the solidity of their romance. So I have them thinking back to a time when they were walking along a beach in St. Tropez, a lovely time when they were young and first in love.

> "I heard la—da da da—da da da—as we walked on the sand
> I heard la—da da da—I believe it was early September
> Through the crash of the waves I could tell that the words were
>   romantic
> Something about sharing
> Something about always
> Tho' the years race along I still think of our song on the sand
> And I still try and search for the words I can barely remember
> Tho' the time tumbles by there is one thing that I
>   am forever certain of
> I hear la—da da da—da da da—da da da—da da da
> And I'm young and in love."

There is something so human, too, about people who can hum "our song," but not remember the words. That little detail is perfect for those two characters. At the same time, it is something that anyone can identify with.

Of course I had to use my own memories and my own impressions of beauty and youth in order to write that song. I was probably remembering my father and mother when they were young, walking along a country road at our summer camp on Stissing Lake. I know I was also thinking about my own summers on Fire Island, walking on the sand with someone I cared for.

I have always loved the beach. I love the feel of the sand and the sound of the waves crashing. I think there is something so romantic about two people—not two men, but *any* two people in love—holding hands and walking on the beach. That song can be anybody's song.

Our wild success in Boston filtered back to New York, so our opening night audience on Broadway already knew they were at a hit musical. They were with us from the thrilling opening—and they stayed with us to the end.

There was something special, though, about the standing ovation that the audience gave to George Hearn when he finished singing "I Am What I Am" at the end of Act One. In a way, it was even more heartwarming than the big ovations for showstoppers like "Hello, Dolly!" and "Mame," because those numbers were huge spectacles, with forty people on stage. This was one man, alone on stage, delivering an honest, heartfelt statement that wiped out the audience. That opening night, when Albin ripped off his wig and marched up the aisle and out of the theater, I felt that I had written the most triumphant song of my career.

It was an ecstatic moment and the house went wild. We didn't even have to do a second act to have a hit.

AND THEN WE found ourselves at the 1984 Tony Awards, where we won six awards. That was an extraordinary evening. People still talk about it.

There were two separate camps in the theater community that year. One group was for the traditional American musical and they wanted *La Cage aux Folles* to win Best Musical. The other group was for the avant-garde musical and they wanted Stephen Sondheim's *Sunday in the Park with George* to win.

Each show had its own group of supporters. But when *La Cage* swept the awards and won for Best Musical, it seemed clear to me that a majority of theater people were voting for traditional musical values. I said as much in my acceptance speech, when I expressed my delight that there was still a place in our business for the simple, melodic musical.

That's what I said and that's what I meant, so it shocked me when my plain and honest statement was perceived by some people as an attack on Stephen Sondheim.

Every now and then the rumor pops up that Stephen Sondheim and I are enemies. That's ridiculous, because we barely know each other. Of the Broadway composers who are still active, I consider him the genius of the group. I respect his work and I hope he respects mine, but as writers our goals are entirely different. We aim at different targets and we usually hit our marks.

These differences are what make our work interesting. I have always felt that an eclectic theater is the healthiest, most exciting kind of musical theater in the world. I would love to see a Stephen Sondheim musical playing across the street from a Kander and Ebb musical, down the block from a Jerome Kern revival and with some avant-garde musical by John La Chiusa around the corner. I don't want everybody to write the same way.

I think that rumor of a feud started before the Tony Awards, back when *Sunday in the Park* first opened. Frank Rich, who was the very powerful theater critic of The New York *Times* at that time, lost his mind over that show and wrote a wild, passionate rave. Practically every week after that, there was at least one article in the *Times* about Sondheim, the show, the director, the stars, the costume designer, maybe even the stage doorman.

Meanwhile, *La Cage* had become this monster hit. It would eventually join *Dolly!* and *Mame* and run over 1,500 performances, making me the only composer-lyricist in American musical theater history with that accomplishment. But you couldn't find a word about our show in the *Times*. After a while, people started asking us what we had done to make them give us the cold shoulder. Finally, after the show had been running about six months to sold-out houses, *finally* we got a feature.

It must have become an embarrassment to the *Times*. It just didn't look good for them to go on ignoring this major hit because their Broadway critic had another agenda.

I never felt there was any personal conflict between Frank Rich and Jerry Herman. He wrote a perfectly decent notice for *La Cage*, especially of my work. It was just that I represented the traditional school of Broadway songwriting and he was an advocate of the new musical styles. Obviously, people in the business didn't agree with him because they chose to give *La Cage* six Tony Awards.

For all my years in show business, I can say that I have never had a problem with a particular critic. In fact, there are some members of the press I feel I can always count on for support and friendship. Liz Smith is one of those people. We co-hosted a benefit together at Carnegie Hall and had the best time. I have always been treated beautifully by critics like Walter Kerr and Clive Barnes in New York and Shirley Eder in Detroit and Ed Wilson of the *Wall Street Journal*. Columnists like Rex Reed and Raidy Harris have always been enthusiastic about my work.

LATER THAT YEAR, *Jerry's Girls* opened on Broadway. The origins of that show went back to 1981, when a man named Larry Alford came to me about doing a retrospective of my work. I had always wanted to write some kind of musical tribute saluting all the women who had ever been in my shows. So we got the idea of doing a revue in which all the performers were women—even the conductor.

Once we had that idea, we got dates and booked the revue at my friend Ted Hook's On Stage, a popular supper club on West Forty-sixth Street in the theater district. The first show featured four girls and a trio of female musicians. The revue got a rave from John Wilson in the New York *Times* and became such a hot ticket that it ran and ran and ran, just like that first little show of mine called *Nightcap*.

The Broadway producer Zev Bufman took it out across the country in February 1984 with Carol Channing, Leslie Uggams, and Andrea McArdle. That production got such good reviews and did such great business that he brought it into New York in December of 1985, with Chita Rivera, Leslie Uggams, and Dorothy Loudon.

What a trio I had!

Leslie is a rare creature. She has a fantastic musical instrument and at the same time is one of the nicest human beings on the planet. There is no ego there, just talent. There's a very strong bond between Leslie and me and her husband, Grahame. As for Chita, I don't know whether to call that lady a great singer, a great dancer, or a great actress, because she is all three. She's not a snooty star, either. Chita is a real pal to everybody in the business—Broadway's favorite trouper. Dorothy is quite a package, too, an inspired and original comedienne with a warm, heartbreaking voice. In all my years of listening for laughter in the theater, I never heard anything like the riots that Dorothy set off with her two solos, "Have a Nice Day" and "Take It All Off."

That production of *Jerry's Girls* got the kind of notices you dream about. Shirley Herz, the terrific lady who was our press agent, counted twenty-two rave reviews from the New York critics. Clive Barnes said that "it should run at least forever," and one of the other reviewers called me "the Norman Rockwell of popular music." But it got a pan from Frank Rich.

* * *

JERRY'S GIRLS HAS always been a popular show on tour, but for some reason, it became an absolute phenomenon in Australia. The show went out in 1987 in a production directed by Larry Alford and it ran for two years. It had barely closed before there was a demand to bring it back. So it went right back and became Australia's biggest hit.

Meanwhile, *La Cage* was spreading its wings in all directions. National companies of the show seemed to be going out every other day, and singers were rushing to record singles of my showtunes, which was highly unusual for the mid–1980s, when everybody was doing rock albums. Gloria Gaynor had a big hit with a disco version of "I Am What I Am," and Perry Como did beautiful recordings of "The Best of Times" and "Song on the Sand."

"Song on the Sand" is a song about the memories that lovers share. Shortly after *La Cage* opened, I met my friend Marty. And for the next seven and a half years, I had someone to share the special moments of my life.

FIFTEEN

"I'll Be Here Tomorrow"

I MET MARTY Finkelstein during one of the happiest periods of my life, at the height of *La Cage*'s incredible success on Broadway. What a fabulous time that was! I was happy being in New York again and spending all my nights on the town. It was the holiday season, so there were always parties to go to after the show. And that's where I met my Marty, at a Christmas party.

I don't remember which friend introduced us, but I do remember somebody pulling me across the room and saying, "Jerry, I want you to meet Marty Finkelstein." We both said our how-do-you-do's and I found myself smiling at this very sweet-looking man with lovely warm eyes and a handsome mustache which he happened to be a tiny bit vain about.

We wandered over to the bar and got two Cokes. (That is just so typical—somehow I always manage to find the one other non-boozer in every crowd.) I felt very comfortable right away with Marty. We took our Cokes and found a seat, and we talked and talked for two hours straight. I felt as if I already knew this man.

After our lovely long conversation, I invited Marty, who lived in Philadelphia, to spend a weekend with me in New York. We would go to the theater, eat dinner in some nice restaurants, and have fun. He accepted my invitation so quickly, and with such enthusiasm, I realized that something was happening. I didn't know exactly what, but I had a feeling that I was going to have a relationship with this young man.

That was the beginning of a remarkable experience that made my life so much richer. I'll never know what made it so special, but we liked each other from that very first moment. We just clicked. For some reason, we found something absolutely irresistible in each other that made our relationship work until the day he died.

Once I realized that this was not going to be an ordinary relationship, I became terribly conscious of how difficult it was going to be to make it work.

I was in a position in my life where I did not have to compromise on just about anything. Suddenly I found myself with another human being who needed and deserved his own place in the sun. It is not easy to be me and have a relationship with somebody who is, let's say, a tie salesman at Bullock's. It is not easy for either party in the relationship. If I wanted this friendship, I could not allow this man to live in my shadow. I would have to find a way to make Marty feel like a *mensch*.

WHEN YOU ARE successful, people treat you like a celebrity. They are always coming up to you and asking your opinion on everything. "You're the expert," they say, "so tell us what's happened to the musical theater." Or they ask you what's wrong with this show or that movie. That can be terribly flattering. But when people pay you that kind of attention all the time, you can become very sure of yourself and develop this sense of certainty about *all* your opinions. Whether you mean to do it or not, you start thinking you know it all.

Marty made me more aware of this. He helped me not to be too full of myself. I didn't ever want to talk down to him because I respected him and I really cared for him. And I didn't have to play the big shot with him because he truly respected and cared for me. Being considerate of Marty taught me to talk to everybody like a person, not like an expert. I found that helped me in all my other relationships, too.

That's what Marty did for me. He taught me how to listen to other people's opinions and how to respect them, even when I didn't particularly agree with them. He was a wonderful person and he was very, very good for me.

The closest Marty and I ever came to a fight was over *Grease*. Marty thought it was charming. I couldn't sit through the thing. I just couldn't bear it. I tried to make allowances for the generation gap, because there was a twenty-year difference in our ages. If I were his age maybe I would have thought *Grease* was adorable. But I wasn't his age, and I hated the show.

Actually, we wound up having interesting talks about our different tastes. I would play *Gypsy* and say to him, "Now, here is a piece of work that is *worthy* of admiration and respect." I would pull out *The King and I* and explain what makes it such a wonderful score. He was very sensitive, and it gave me great pleasure to watch him respond to the music I loved.

At the same time, I learned an awful lot about pop music from Marty. He introduced me to this pop composer named Dan Fogelberg, who wrote a couple of gorgeous songs that I really love. One of Dan Fogelberg's songs from the 1970s, "Longer Than," sort of became "our" song. I hadn't known a thing about that kind of music and Marty taught me to be more open to it. He left me his huge collection of tapes and CDs when he died, and whenever I listen to one of his albums I always thank him for opening my head to other kinds of music.

As for *Grease*, I wound up saying, "Look, Marty, have a good time with it. Enjoy it. Just please don't play it when I'm in the house."

*   *   *

ONE BIG REASON our relationship worked was because Marty and I had so much in common, especially our interest in architecture and design. In Philadelphia, Marty worked at design and restoration, the same sort of thing that I was doing in New York and California, and he was wonderful at that work. He had also designed a public fountain, a very nice piece of work that he was justifiably proud of.

After we had been together for a while, I thought of a way for us to work together that would be great fun and also respect his individual creative talent. "Marty," I said to him, "have you ever been to Key West?" He said that he hadn't, but that he had always wanted to.

"Let's get on a plane and fly down there for a few days," I said. "I want to show you some old houses down there that you will love. They are exactly what you and I should get our hands into."

So we flew down to Key West for a long weekend and I showed Marty all the things I loved—the little bridges, the tree-lined streets, the charming old houses. There is something very romantic about the ambience and informality of Key West. Marty was so enchanted, he absolutely fell in love with the place. From that moment, he was a changed person. He couldn't wait to go back, and in fact, he moved there for good a year later.

Our first project together was restoring these two Colonial houses smack in the middle of Old Town. They were sister houses built side by side in 1898, just opposite the pink library on Fleming Street. They were huge places and quite splendid, but they had been let go and were very shabby when we bought them. What we did was more restoration than renovation. We kept the original architecture intact, because these were historic places, but we made them look like new houses.

First, we made everything structurally sound and then we put in magnificent doors and crown molding and beautiful golden flooring. Architecturally, everything was authentic, down to the last little detail. We put our modernization work into the bathrooms and kitchens, which were right up to the minute in style and efficiency, and then we had these magnificent pools installed out back. We didn't even stop there—we put in lawns and planted trees and landscaped the whole area.

Those first two houses we restored sold instantly, so we bought a third house and moved into that one while we worked on it. By this time we had started our own business. It was called Majer Design—MA for Marty and JER for Jerry—and it was very successful.

The preservation society loved us. A lot of people buy these old Victorian houses and jazz them up, but we honestly restored them by keeping the integrity of the original design. All together, we restored eleven houses and won several architectural awards for our designs. Some of the houses we did were no more than falling-down shacks, so we rescued them and created elegant new exteriors for them. Not only did the business make money and earn professional respect, but Marty and I also had terrific fun working together.

We did nine more projects in Key West. Marty moved into one house that we were working on and I moved into another one right next door. He was a young man and it was good for him to have his independence. He decorated his home to his own taste without big brother Jerry looking over his shoulder. He could have his own friends over and invite his mother and father to come down and visit him in his own home. And I was able to say to friends of mine, "Come down and spend the weekend with me at my house in Key West."

It was nice to have that privacy. But the truth was, we were always in each other's houses. We would have breakfast at my house, and Marty was in my pool every day. When nobody was around I would be sitting on Marty's living room floor about five nights a week, watching television with him. We didn't even have to walk around to the front door to visit; we just walked through the fence.

Marty loved Key West. He had a lot of friends that I didn't even know down there, and he became involved in the local life. Key West became his town.

That was such a wonderful time for me. I was completely fulfilled, creatively and personally. I had this incredible hit show on Broadway and I had Marty and the houses in Key West. Having this person in my life made an amazing difference. It was the best of times and we were having just the *best* time.

THE ONLY THING that marred our wonderful life was the shadow of AIDS that was moving over us. Many of our friends started to get ill during these years and some of them died. In that sense, it was a very hard time because we knew that something awful was happening all around us.

We had been together about five years when, one terrible day, Marty came down with a bronchial infection. It wouldn't go away, so we went to the hospital in Key West. I was with Marty in his hospital room when the doctor came in and told us what it was.

Next to the death of my mother, that was the toughest moment in my life. I wanted so much to be supportive, but I broke down. I remember standing over this little sink in his hospital room and crying my heart out. I was hysterical with grief. Marty wound up supporting me. "It's all right, Jerry," he kept saying to me. "It's going to be all right." In that terrible moment, he was not thinking about himself, about his own condition, but about me, about how I felt. I'll never forget that about Marty, because that was the kind of person he was.

Marty lived two and a half years from that day, and I am happy to say that he was quite well during those years, right to the end. And it *was* all right, just the way he said. We had great fun during those two and a half years and we never let his illness ruin our time together. We stayed in Key West, which he loved more than any place in the world, and we threw lots of parties. I also became very close to his family in Philadelphia, who accepted me with open arms like another son. I am still very close to them.

Marty was in Philadelphia when the end came. He was visiting his family when he got another bout of this pneumonia and fungus in the chest. I went down and stayed so I could be with him constantly in his hospital room in case he needed me. He was on all these tubes and breathing things, and if he needed something done, I wanted to be the one who would do it.

One day, the doctor came in and leveled with all of us in the family. "He just doesn't have enough of an immune system to fight this thing any more," he told us. And that was the end.

The funeral was very hard. It was so difficult to understand why we had to bear this handsome, charming, wonderful human being—only thirty-six years old—to his grave. It makes you really wonder what the whole thing is about. The *why* of it.

When my mother died at forty-four years of age, I asked myself, "What is this all about? How can it be that Ruth Herman will never see my first Broadway show?" And on the opening night of every one of my shows I would stand in the back and say, "Why is Ruth not here? How can she not be here? It's not right. It's not fair."

I feel the same way about Marty. I keep asking myself, "Why

did he have to leave? Why did he have to leave so *soon?*" There isn't a person alive who hasn't asked themselves that. You question it and you question it, but you never get an answer.

I WANTED SO much to leave something in Marty's name. Something permanent that would be a help to others, because that's what he would have wanted. So I helped create a hospice in Key West called Marty's Place.

Marty's Place was made out of an old motel. It has individual units, so each private home has its own kitchen and bath and a bedroom where the residents can bring their own possessions. There's a beautiful swimming pool with lawn chairs and plantings of tropical foliage. We just added three new units and the place is still growing. It is one of the most successfully run homes in the world for people with AIDS and has become a model for other hospices. It gives me a feeling of great sadness and yet enormous pleasure to drive by that handsome compound and see this forest-green sign with gold letters out front that says Marty's Place.

It took me time to get over Marty's death—and no, you never really "get over" the death of someone who is close and dear to you like that. I still feel the shock of losing my best friend Carol Dorian at Christmastime in 1992. I am still numb from that loss. To lose your oldest and dearest friend overnight—the person you call first thing in the morning practically every day of your life—without having the chance to prepare or even to say goodbye, that is a very hard thing.

Those first years after Marty was gone were not easy in any way. AIDS was running rampant by then, and more and more friends were dying. I was very hard hit when the man I called my brother, my dear friend and collaborator, Michael Stewart, died of complications from lupus. I even lost my beloved pet, my wonderful cat named Barnaby, during that same horrible period. That winter of 1992 was the worst of times.

PEOPLE DON'T ALWAYS understand how hard it is to be the survivor. Along with the terrible grief, you feel so lost and disoriented. I would sit there alone, rattling around in my beautiful, empty brownstone on East Sixty-first Street, waiting for people who never came. From time to time I would look up, expecting to see Carol coming through the door with her famous cookies. Or I would think I heard Barnaby jumping up on the sink for a drink of water from the faucet. I kept expecting a phone call from Mike Stewart, all thrilled about some new theater project. Most of all, I kept waiting for Marty to come home.

One of the hardest things I had to do was sell the house in Key West. I tried to do it with my chin up, but it was very painful for me to pack up and close forever what had been a very lovely part of my life. After Marty died, I struggled for three years to maintain my own life down there, but I was not happy about it. I didn't want the pool man or the gardener, and I didn't want the empty house.

I hated to say goodbye to everything that Key West had meant to me because I hate any kind of ending. I would like it if the show business that I knew and loved in the 1960s could just go on and on. I would like it if every person I had ever known and loved could just go on living. I want everything in the world to be pink and blue and yellow and to go on forever.

There is a song in *Mack and Mabel* called "I Promise You a Happy Ending" that Mack Sennett sings to Mabel when she is at her lowest.

"I promise you a happy ending
Like the ones that you see on the screen
So if you've had a bad beginning
Love will come out winning
In the closing scene
And when you find it rough contending
With the grind that the world puts us through
I can promise you a happy ending
That has you loving me
Loving you."

I needed someone to say that to me when the day came for me to go to my own doctor and say, "My lover recently died of AIDS. Shouldn't I be tested?" He said to me, "I was going to suggest it myself." So I went to get tested and I found out that I was HIV-positive.

After all my losses I now felt my own mortality sitting like a dark cloud over my head. It was a very, very difficult time.

I CAN'T SAY that after Marty's death I took comfort in my work, because I was not writing at that time. After I lost Marty I just didn't feel like writing for a while. I didn't know what I felt like doing.

The other big reason I wasn't writing was because I had been spoiled by *La Cage aux Folles*. That had been such a joyous experience—the crowning glory of my career—that I was very hesitant about following it up. I was offered everything under the sun, but I turned them all down because they all seemed so pallid after *La Cage*.

I must have been handed *Pocketful of Miracles* about twenty times. That is the charming Damon Runyon story about a poor lady named Apple Annie who pretends to be rich. It is definitely material for a musical, and I might have done that show in 1954, or even 1964. But I had gone beyond that kind of material and I honestly didn't know how to go back to a simple musical idea like that.

I feel the same way today. I am still turning things down because I don't want to do a musical with less substance than *Dear World* or *La Cage*. There is no pleasure in that for me.

I was recently offered *Bullets Over Broadway*, which I thought was a hilarious film. I saw it twice and I laughed myself silly. I admire Woody Allen's work tremendously. His film is an absolute delight and it certainly has the *tone* of a musical. I just didn't want to musicalize it because I didn't think there was anything in the material to sing about.

To me, what makes a musical are larger-than-life characters who have something important to say. I can write passionate musical statements like "If He Walked Into My Life" and "I Am What I Am" and "Before the Parade Passes By" for people with dimension. But if you don't have that kind of character to write for, why would you want to put yourself through the grind of writing a Broadway musical?

THE DECADE THAT started so beautifully for me ended so tragically that I felt as if I had finally fallen *off* the roller coaster.

During the five years that *La Cage* was running, I was the toast of the town. For the seven and a half years that it lasted, my relationship with Marty was the joy of my life. I had my friends, I had my houses, I had everything. But by the late 1980s and into the early '90s, when my friends were dying, it seemed to me that all these losses coincided with the death of the American musical theater.

That was the time when I packed myself up, moved back to California for good, and pivotally changed my life.

That was not an easy move for me. I had been living in my East Side townhouse for more than a decade. Everything I owned and cherished was in that house, and everything I loved about the theater was right across town on Broadway. How could I pull up these deep roots and move away for good?

I do not take change lightly, even though I am in a business where most people flit around without giving it a thought. Jule Styne, for example, had something like thirty-four publishers. I am probably the only person in show business who has kept the same agent, the same law firm, and the same publisher for my entire career.

At that time in my life, any change at all upset me because it felt like another loss, and I really couldn't take more loss. Even in terms of my health, which so far had been steady, thank God, any change would only mean deterioration. I just wanted everything to stay the same.

So I had another one of those talks with myself. "Jerry," I said, "you have had it all. If there is nothing left for you to do, at least you can enjoy what you've got. Maybe it's time to buy another lovely house in California, put your feet up, and be happy."

Honestly, I had no intention of having a second career or making some kind of comeback by moving out here. I was resigned to retiring gracefully. All I was looking for was the perfect spot to set down my rocking chair.

This place I am living in now is the home of homes. I call it my mansion, and I had to beat my accountant over the head before he let me buy it from David Wolper, the film producer. David was moving to Napa Valley where he had bought a great deal of acreage so he could build a house with a private golf course. But he had to sell his mansion in Bel Air, which is 18,000 square feet, and find a smaller pied à terre to use when he came to L.A.

David liked my place and I loved his, so we sort of *swapped* our two houses. At the same time, I sold my beloved New

York townhouse to Sally Jessy Raphael, so everything turned out just fine.

HOW COULD ANYBODY not be happy in this idyllic place? I wish everybody could see what I see when I open my eyes in the morning—golden California sunshine streaming through the French doors of my bedroom, miles of gorgeous vistas, flowers blooming all around the swimming pool, fresh fruit on the breakfast table set up on the patio, and flocks of birds sitting in a 200-year-old pin oak tree, singing their hearts out. It is blissful here.

In my den, there is a huge model of a ship that has been traveling with me from house to house for thirty-two years. It was the first frivolous thing that I ever acquired and it has special meaning for me because I bought it during a very exciting time in my life. We were in the process of getting *Milk and Honey* ready for its Broadway opening and I was out taking a walk one day in Greenwich Village, feeling very happy and upbeat.

I was strolling down Greenwich Avenue when I passed a little antique shop and saw this beautiful ship model, all rough and weatherbeaten, sitting by itself in the window. I don't know why, but something about it just attracted me. The very crudeness of it was appealing. And all that careful, meticulous handiwork. Maybe it reminded me of all the detail that goes into my own work that nobody really sees.

I found out that the captain of a tugboat had made this ship out of odd bits and pieces. You could imagine him, all alone at night in his cabin, carving all the little lifeboats, twisting all the little ropes. I said to the shop owner, "I would like to have that." I didn't even ask how much it cost and I don't even remember how much I paid.

Wherever that piece is, that's my home.

* * *

I HAVE MY own way of entertaining myself in this paradise. When friends come over, we still have the best times at the piano, or just sitting and talking around the dining room table. My big music room is a wonderful place for parties or for watching movies on the big screen. Downstairs, I have a game room with antique pinball machines and slot machines and all kinds of toys. Eliza Doolittle would also love it that in every room in the house there are lots of chocolates for me to eat. And of course, I am always playing music.

What gives me great pleasure is playing not just the scores I have always loved, but also things I haven't heard in a long time. I am just crazy about this show called *A Tree Grows in Brooklyn,* by Arthur Schwartz and Dorothy Fields. That show was their *Mack and Mabel*—it should have been the big one for them, but for some reason it never happened. I just love that show with all my heart, and I often find myself playing "I'll Buy You a Star" and "Make the Man Love Me" and other songs from that score.

Some of my deepest pleasures are close to home. Jane Dorian Haspel and her husband David moved into a lovely place within walking distance, and we regularly find ourselves at each other's dinner tables or going to the movies together. My goddaughter Sarah and I have a special relationship. She's five years old and beautiful, with a delicious twenty-year-old mentality. Sarah lights up when Uncle Jerry greets her, and Uncle Jerry is, very simply, knocked out by her.

One day, at one of those formal tea parties that Sarah loves to have in my garden, Jane and David asked me if I would let the Starbright Pediatric Foundation honor me with a fundraiser. Knowing the fine work that organization does to help terminally ill children, I agreed—expecting a nice dinner with a lot of long speeches in some hotel ballroom.

Cut to June 30, 1993. The Hollywood Bowl!

A crowd of 11,000 people cheering like they were at a football game, including all my New York friends who had flown in to be there. The entire ninety-piece Los Angeles Philharmonic, thrillingly conducted by Don Pippin. Memorable performances by Bea Arthur, Michael Feinstein, Rita Moreno, Davis Gaines, Florence Lacey, Karen Morrow, Lee Roy Reams, Leslie Uggams, Lorna Luft—and George Hearn, in the eleven o'clock spot, flattening out the place with "I Am What I Am." Liza, Angela, Paul and Linda McCartney appeared via satellite. Carol Channing closed the first act to cheers by descending an endless staircase in her Dolly finery. I came down those same stairs at the very end to do "The Best of Times" with the entire company, with a chorus of 11,000 humming along. And to top it all off—fireworks!

Greg Willenborg produced the entire extravaganza with taste and flair, and it was aired on PBS a few months later. As I said twenty-five years earlier in Sardi's, *Wow!* What a crowning end to a career—I thought.

But you know, the funniest thing happened when I was quietly enjoying my so-called retirement. My rocking chair turned into a roller coaster—and my career took off again!

SO MANY THINGS started happening. I am not exactly sure where it all began. I certainly got a lift from the lovely album that RCA Victor brought out in 1992, with Don Pippin conducting the RCA Victor Symphony Orchestra on *Jerry Herman's Broadway*. And I adored collaborating with Michael Feinstein on his 1993 album, *Michael Feinstein Sings the Jerry Herman Songbook*. I had found in Michael a singer who truly understood my style, and accompanying him felt very natural and right. When we recorded that album we found ourselves breathing together. I was truly saddened when the project came to an end.

You never really know how the energy builds up. All I know is, I was suddenly busier than I had ever been in my life.

One day I got a call from the producer Manny Kladitus, asking if I would once more supervise a revival of *Hello, Dolly!*—a really big one, celebrating the show's thirtieth anniversary and starring my darling Carol Channing. My old friend Mark Reiner did the casting and the brilliant direction was by my pal Lee Roy Reams. That show started out on what was supposed to be a limited national tour in 1994, but by the time it came into the Lunt-Fontanne Theater on Broadway the following year, it had been booked overseas in Japan and Australia and about a million other places. It was a major production and a phenomenal success.

My job was to oversee all the details of the show so that it looked exactly like the original. But I had to make a few significant changes, because the original show and our *memories* of the original show were not always the same. That's because we remember things the way we *want* them to be, not the way they actually were.

Everybody remembers, for example, the famous scene when Dolly makes her entrance at the top of that magnificent staircase at the Harmonia Gardens. The truth is, that original staircase was not at all magnificent. In fact, it was straight and short and it was made out of *cardboard!* But because Dolly's entrance down those stairs has become legendary, people are absolutely certain that they saw her coming down a grand staircase.

So that's what I gave them in the revival—the grand, gorgeous staircase they *think* they saw. We bowed the staircase to give it more dimension and added all those iron curlicues. Then we covered the handrails in velvet and strung lights up the stairs. People also remember the "Before the Parade Passes By" number as being much more elaborate than it actually was, so I strung another garland of lights to keep that illusion.

Carol was the one who convinced me to go along with that production, and I have to admit that I was delighted but also a little amazed when it turned into such a major theatrical event. Carol herself was the biggest amazement. She has always been a dear, dear friend, but I couldn't believe my eyes when I saw her on stage. Here she was, almost seventy-five years old, and she was truly wonderful—better than she ever was. The critics not only recognized her comic genius, but they also said that her interpretation of the role was much deeper and more poignant.

People went *crazy* for that show. I never saw a show with so many standing ovations. Even in New York, the reviews said it was a reminder of the kind of fresh, innocent, exuberant musicals that you don't find on Broadway anymore. Carol was in seventh heaven and my heart almost broke with joy on opening night to see that the Broadway audience still adores those big, old-fashioned, entertaining shows that I write.

Then, Jon Wilner and Peter LeDonne finally raised the money with Laura and John Pomerantz for that London revival of my dream show, *Mack and Mabel.* That was like a fantasy come true for me because I finally got to see that show done the way it was meant to be—and because I helped to make it happen.

So much in this chapter of my life has been about getting a second chance at life. I began taking a new medication that my doctor felt was extremely promising. Not only was *Mack and Mabel* getting a second chance, *I* was getting a second chance. How many second chances do you get in this business? You don't!

*   *   *

ALL OF A sudden, people were rediscovering me and my music. I recently flew to New York to receive the Oscar Hammerstein Award from the York Theater Company, and it turned out to be one of the most gratifying experiences of my whole career. It made me feel so good to receive such meaningful recognition from my peers—and the party was a blast.

Angela Lansbury was the honorary chairman of the event, Carol Channing made the presentation, and Don Pippin and Lee Roy Reams put together a star-studded concert that had people standing on their chairs. That whole evening was terrifically emotional for me. I am still glowing from it.

At the very end of the show, the entire cast came out to join me in singing "The Best of Times." Once more, I turned to Carol Channing and very quietly said, "What can possibly happen next?"

ACTUALLY, A LOT of things are happening again, because I am not afraid to take a chance on doing something brand-new! I had never worked in television before and the challenge to do something new really stimulated my creative juices.

Mrs. Santa Claus, this project that Angela Lansbury asked me to do with her, is giving me great pleasure. And it's a joy to be working with Angie again. And now *Mame* has been optioned for a three-hour Hallmark Hall of Fame TV special, so it looks like my affair with television is no flash in the pan. But I think I really arrived when I was asked to write the theme song for Barney, the purple dinosaur.

I have also become very involved in charity work, doing AIDS benefits all over the country with people like Oprah Winfrey, Angela Lansbury, Tommy Tune, and Elizabeth Taylor. One of the things I did for Tuesday's Child, which is a wonderful organization that helps children with AIDS, was this huge concert of *Mame*, beautifully put together by my good friend John Bowab, with three different Mames: Janis Paige, Nancy Dussault, and Juliet Prowse.

And in the middle of all this, I even got involved with a new boyfriend. So much for retirement!

IF I WERE asked to look back at my life and choose the absolute highlights—what Comden and Green brilliantly refer to as "The real stuff in life to cling to"—my answer would surprisingly have very little to do with show business or songwriting. I would say: knowing that my own medical records will help many others to manage their illness and live longer and happier lives. I would say: my beautiful memories of people I loved, Carol Dorian, Marty Finkelstein, and Ruth Herman. I would say: knowing that my presence on this earth might have changed even a few people's prejudices and perceptions of gays. And heading the list, I would say my lifelong friendships—giving love and getting it back in such abundance.

I HATE TO let this book go, because every day new things are happening to me that make me happy to be alive, and I want to record them.

This morning I jumped out of bed and came out here to my garden to sit in the sun and think about all the exciting things I have planned for this day. I plan to go to a rehearsal of *Mrs. Santa Claus*. Then it will be time for me to do a magazine interview. *Variety* called me "the musical-theater man of the moment," which gives me a big kick.

Sheila bought some Dungeness crabs for lunch, but first I need to call New York to talk with my marvelous agent, Biff Liff, about a leading lady for this television version of *Mame*. I also have to unpack from my marvelous trip to the University of Miami, where I opened the new Jerry Herman Ring Theater that they named for me.

Later this morning, my physical trainer will be coming to the house to take me through my workout. My doctor called first thing this morning with great news about my T-cell count. My counts have quadrupled since this new medication, so I have all this new energy.

I was part of a group that was put on a protease inhibitor and it has made all the difference in my life. When my counts shot up so dramatically, it made me realize that there is true hope out there for everyone. It convinced me that AIDS is a disease that can be controlled. The success of this new protocol has helped to get the drug approved by the FDA so it can be put on the market for others. Along with all my AIDS fundraising work, this was one of the most meaningful things I have ever done.

After lunch, I want to drive into town to look at the new suits at Neiman Marcus on Wilshire. And maybe I'll pick up some chocolates at See's.

Now that *Mack and Mabel* has been rescued from oblivion, people are talking about reviving *Dear World*. Before Robert E. Lee died, he and his collaborator Jerry Lawrence had actually worked on a new script that we called *The Madwoman*. It's a tighter, more concise, and I think a much better version. We won't need a huge chorus or a twenty-six-piece orchestra and we can use a set with real imagination. I have a meeting scheduled in my book about that project.

Jane, David, and Sarah are coming over for dinner, so I'll have to check with Sheila about what time and all that. But when my guests leave, I want to look at a script that just arrived from my agent. I am still looking for that perfect piece of material to start working on for my next show, and maybe today will be the day that I find it.

Whatever this new day brings, I am optimistic that it will be something wonderful. I have always been a positive thinker because I honestly believe that:

> "The best of times is now
> What's left of summer but a faded rose?
> The best of times is now
> As for tomorrow, well who knows, who knows, who knows?
> So hold this moment fast
> And live and love as hard as you know how
> And make this moment last
> Because the best of times is now, is now, is now. . . ."

Early in my career people used to put me down for writing upbeat songs—as if the feelings I put into them were not genuine. It has taken me the better part of my lifetime to make people understand that I write the way I feel, and that these sentiments are honest. We all have to write from our own life experience and be true to those feelings. I can't help writing melodic showtunes that are bouncy, buoyant, and optimistic. That's me. And I am what I am.

This morning, when I walked out to my garden and looked up at the sun, I felt the same joy and excitement that I did all those years ago when I woke up in my first apartment to begin my new life. And I had to smile, because I thought I could hear my mother saying: "It's today!"

Index